Relationships and Well-Being Over the Life Stages

Relationships and Well-Being Over the Life Stages

Pat M. Keith & Robert B. Schafer

PRAEGER

New York
Westport, Connecticut
London

HQ
536
.K37
1991

Library of Congress Cataloging-in-Publication Data

Keith, Pat M.
   Relationships and well-being over the life stages / Pat M. Keith,
Robert B. Schafer.
     p.   cm.
   Includes bibliographical references and index.
   ISBN 0–275–93422–5 (alk. paper)
   1. Family—United States. 2. Marriage—United States. 3. Sex
role—United States. 4. Quality of life—United States. 5. Life
cycle, Human. I. Schafer, Robert B. II. Title.
HQ536.K37   1991
306.8—dc20   91–11078

British Library Cataloguing in Publication Data is available.

Library of Congress Catalog Card Number: 91–11078
ISBN: 0–275–93422–5

First published in 1991

Praeger Publishers, One Madison Avenue, New York, NY 10010
An imprint of Greenwood Publishing Group, Inc.

Printed in the United States of America

The paper used in this book complies with the
Permanent Paper Standard issued by the National
Information Standards Organization (Z39.48–1984).

10 9 8 7 6 5 4 3 2 1

For our families and colleagues who have contributed
to our well-being
and for Rita, who meant so much to us

Contents

Illustrations

Tables

Figure

Acknowledgments

A number of people and organizations helped in the development and preparation of this book. The data collection and early writing were made possible by support from the Science and Education Administration of the United States Department of Agriculture through the Competitive Research Grants Office. We also have benefited from our association with and assistance from the College of Liberal Arts and Sciences Research Institute, the Graduate College, and the Department of Sociology at Iowa State University.

We appreciated Toni Genalo and Hazel Cook of the Iowa State University Statistical Laboratory for their leadership, their expertise in data collection and management, and their unfailing enthusiasm. We could not have had better assistance.

We acknowledge Elisabeth Schafer for her considerable effort and analyses of diet quality in chapter 9. Robbyn Wacker contributed to an earlier review of the literature on gender roles in later life. We thank Ladonna Osborn for her invaluable help in the preparation of the manuscript. We are especially appreciative of the encouragement and patience of the editors at Praeger.

Finally, we are grateful for the support of our families, whose well-being may have been diminished somewhat by our work.

Relationships and Well-Being Over the Life Stages

1

Relationships and Well-Being Over the Life Stages

In this book we consider personal characteristics and family relationships and how they are linked with well-being over the life course. Increasingly, individuals, families, and scholars are seeking to understand how interpersonal behavior may contribute to well-being in a variety of circumstances. From this interest has come the recognition that behavior that seems to facilitate well-being and is rewarding at one life stage may be less productive at others. Furthermore, the contribution of relationships to well-being may vary by personal and social circumstances. These personal and social circumstances often reflect the stage or period of the individual life course or of the family cycle. It is the variation in relationships and well-being for individuals and families in particular stages that is of primary interest here. But relationships between spouses are affected by responses of families to trends in the larger society. Some social trends that especially may shape relationships between spouses and have far-reaching implications for families guide the focus of this book.

Social trends identified as having long-range significance include (1) the increased employment of women, (2) the dramatic growth in single-parent households, (3) heightened attention to the aging of the population and to older families, and (4) changing attitudes toward gender roles (Piotrkowski, Rapoport & Rapoport, 1987). The social, demographic, and economic implications of these changes account for some of the major concerns of the groups investigated in this book. Throughout, the focus is on variation in well-being (e.g., self-concept, role strain, and mental health) over the adult life course and the factors that may foster it at various life stages and in different family situations.

This book offers observations on persons in diverse circumstances across the life course that are often not included in the same research but that will have a profound effect on the structure of American society throughout the rest of this century and into the next. Among the groups and circumstances that are studied and compared are (1) one- and two-job families, (2) single-parent women and their married counterparts, (3) older and younger couples, (4) modern and traditional spouses, and (5) the differential experiences of husbands and wives.

Whereas we are able to make observations about relationships and well-being in these subgroups, we also attend to the salience of life stages for role relationships among married couples. A specific advantage of the information in this book is that the views of both husbands and wives are taken into account. Broader social trends noted previously, such as changes in attitudes toward gender roles and increases in female employment, have potential implications for altered relationships between married partners. For example, these trends may have consequences for marital quality, the division of labor in the household, and conceptions of equity or inequity in the partnership (Spitze, 1988).

ONE- AND TWO-JOB FAMILIES

The increased employment of women shapes the investigation of work-family relationships and leads to the examination of differences in the dynamics and experiences in one- and two-job families. During the first forty years of this century, the major change in the patterns of women's employment was in the type of work they did. The proportion of women employed in clerical and comparable jobs increased, while the proportion working in factories and agriculture declined (Piotrkowski et al., 1987). In the latter half of this century, the labor-force participation of women has doubled and, especially, increasing proportions of young married women with children are employed outside the home. Furthermore, employed women now resemble the majority of the female population. Early in this century women in the labor force were usually young and single, whereas now the majority of women employed outside the home are married (Spitze, 1988). More than 60 percent of married mothers with school-aged children are employed (Piotrkowski et al., 1987). Even so, only about one-half of wives work full time outside the home. Although women have always worked and their numbers likely have been underestimated, "what is a modern phenomenon is the emergence of a predominant family form in which both husbands and wives work outside the home" (Piotrkowski et al., 1987:254).

In the past decade and a half, much research on the paid employment of women has focused on the effects of their involvement in the labor force per se, with less attention to the characteristics of the employment or to variation in the experiences at work (Spitze, 1988). Furthermore, samples that have been studied have been somewhat restrictive; most have been of white, middle-class husband-wife families, neglecting the outcomes of employment for single parents or for minority or working-class families.

Investigation of the consequences of women's employment has followed several themes. Research in the past fifteen years has examined the effects of women's employment on divorce and marital instability, marital quality (including marital satisfaction, life satisfaction, and health), household work and power (including studies of the effect of female employment on housework, marital power, and equity), combined effects of the employment of both spouses, and the effect of maternal employment on children (Spitze, 1988). Information in this book is most closely related to the research themes on marital quality including investigation of disagreement between spouses, satisfaction with work-family roles, evaluation of performance of work-family roles, equity, and indices of mental health. Additional central topics involve household work, including the distribution of labor, its effect on mental health, and concerns with equity.

This book provides insights into both the modern and the more traditional family patterns. Aspects of life that bring satisfaction, feelings of deprivation fostered by a particular family pattern, and factors that may cause strain in both modern and traditional families are examined. For example, factors associated with mental health and self-concept of spouses in both modern and traditional types of families are explored. Such an examination permits consideration of dimensions of the interface between work and family in both traditional and modern patterns. The way in which work and family demands are negotiated in two-spouse families and managed in single-parent families will remain a critical issue for both in the years to come. In chapters 3 and 8 a glimpse of work-family life in both types of households is provided.

SINGLE-PARENT FAMILIES

Changing family structures are reflected in increases in single-parent families. The change has been especially graphic since 1970. From the middle of the nineteenth century until the 1970s, about 10 percent of American families were managed by a single mother or father (Gongla & Thompson, 1987). In a little over a decade, the proportion of families with children under 18 in which there was only one parent increased from 10 percent to a little over 20 percent of families with dependent children in the household. Single-parent families, which have increased the most rapidly of any family form except cohabitating couples, have grown at twenty-one times the rate of two-spouse families. Another way to view the increase is to note that single-parent families increased by 107 percent during the 1970s, while traditional two-parent families decreased by 4 percent. Thus, there has been a marked increase in both the absolute and the relative number of single-parent families (Gongla & Thompson, 1987). Furthermore, the absolute number of single-parent families at any one time does not include all of those who have been part of a single-parent household at some point in their lives.

It is anticipated that the number and proportion of single parents will continue to increase. Gongla and Thompson (1987) observe that any reduction in the number of single-parent families composed of formerly married women probably will be replaced by families with dependent children that are maintained by never-married women.

Thus, the influence of this family pattern is projected to be far reaching; for example, Norton and Glick (1986) estimate that about 60 percent of all children born in 1986 will live about one year or longer in a single-parent home before they reach age 18. Increasingly then, children are likely to spend part of their childhood in a single-parent family.

Single-parent families today have different origins than those in an earlier period of time. In previous years, death of a husband was the impetus for most single-parent families; recently, however, divorce and separation have accounted for the majority of these families. Furthermore, these families are younger than previously, and they will continue to rear younger, but fewer, children. Single parents more often than their married peers are employed, but in low-paying jobs (Piotrkowski et al., 1987). Despite the profile of disadvantage that is often used to describe these parents, chapter 8 on single parents presents systematic analyses of aspects of their employment and their reflections on it in relation to self-regard and depressive symptoms. These analyses will give some insights into the impact of work on the well-being and circumstances of these families. Inclusion of single parents allows comparisons of aspects of their lives with those of their married peers in two-job families.

OLDER FAMILIES

There is increasing attention to older families and how they manage their retirement, health, finances, and social ties (Bahr & Peterson, 1989; Brubaker, 1990; Condie, 1989). More than one-half of the older population is married and resides with spouses in independent households. With the expected decline in male death rates in the future, there will be more couples in their middle and later years than there are now.

Even with relatively high divorce rates, it is anticipated that one-fifth of first marriages will last for fifty years or more (Condie, 1989).

There have been relatively few studies of marital relationships among older couples compared to the magnitude of research on younger spouses (Treas & Bengtson, 1987), although families in later life have recently been referred to as a "burgeoning research area" (Brubaker, 1990). A chapter on older families could include most of the topics that might be addressed with younger partners as well as those of particular interest to gerontologists, for example, marital dissolution (including divorce and widowhood), remarriage, childlessness, relationships with siblings and extended family, and caregiving. In chapter 5 we look closely at the marital relationship and at mental health as both have been influenced by orientations toward gender roles and the division of labor in the home.

One question that is often asked about older families but is inapplicable to their younger counterparts concerns the impact of retirement on the relationship between spouses. An exception for middle-aged and younger couples, of course, might be forced retirement caused by physical disability or unemployment. For marital relationships of both younger and older spouses, however, the effects of being attached or unattached to the labor force have been a source of interest.

Involvement in the labor force has changed somewhat for both older married men and women. In a little over two decades (1960–1988), the proportion of married men aged 45 to 64 who were employed decreased from 93 percent to 82 percent (Statistical Abstract of the United States, 1990). During the same time, the proportion of married men aged 65 or over in the labor force decreased from 37 percent to 17.5 percent. As involvement in the labor force declined for middle-aged men, it increased in general for women; for example, between 1960 and 1988, employment of married women aged 35 to 44 increased from 36 to 73 percent and from 34 to 53.7 percent among women aged 45 to 64. There was little increase in the proportion of women who continued to work past age 65, from 6 percent in 1960 to 7.4 percent in 1988. Increases in employment of women result in more families having to address the retirement of both spouses; because few women continue to work beyond age 65, the timing of retirement may take on special importance.

Consequently, the implications of attachment to the labor force are growing more complex as family patterns increasingly differentiate in later life. Increasingly, there will be dual-retired couples in which both spouses will have withdrawn from employment. The resources that these individuals may bring to the retirement process likely will be quite different from those of their peer couples in which only one spouse has retired.

Moreover, decisions regarding the timing of retirement, especially when the women may have entered careers substantially later than their husbands, may affect the personal adjustment of both. As women increasingly are involved in careers, their attitudes and adaptation to retirement also may undergo change. A primary interest in chapter 5 is to determine differences in gender-role attitudes and behavior in younger and older families and their consequences for well-being. We also attend to comparisons of the implications of employment status of both men and women and for their partners in the middle and later years. Szinovacz (1989) noted the importance of studying couples rather than individuals in attempting to assess the adjustment to retirement among older families.

CHANGING GENDER ROLES

Accompanying the demographic and structural changes noted is the transition in traditional gender-role attitudes, although the modification of attitudes has not always been accompanied by altered behavior in the family and in the workplace. Research findings on the directional ordering of attitude-behavior relationships in regard to gender-role attitudes and employment behavior have been contradictory (Blee & Tickamyer, 1987). The dominant trend suggests that changes in work and family life precede changes in gender-role attitudes and beliefs (Losh-Hesselbart, 1987). Changes in attitudes toward gender roles, including increased acceptance of paid employment by females and the involvement of men in the household, is greater among women, younger persons, and groups in better financial circumstances (Scanzoni & Arnett, 1987).

Recently, there has been greater acceptance of the employment of women and of shared child rearing by parents, with a trend toward convergence of work and family attitudes of men and women (Piotrkowski et al., 1987). The latter attitude changes have been reflected in greater psychological involvement of men with their families and increased noneconomic commitments to employment by women. Even so, changes in the family roles of men may lag behind the transitions in the work roles of women. And in other areas, convergence is not found between reported gender-role attitudes and subsequent behavior. Although the involvement òf men in the household might be expected to increase dramatically with retirement, there is little evidence for egalitarianism in this life stage (Szinovacz, 1989).

There is the greatest approval for nontraditional attitudes that are related to the nonfamilial roles of women. Both men and women endorse equal job opportunities and the same pay for the same work. But the public also supports occupational segregation and condones restrictions on combinations of family and paid work for women (Losh-Hesselbart,

1987). For example, the public has expressed a preference for male physicians and police officers and for male bosses. Differences between the responses of men and women on gender-role attitudes depend on the specific items. Men seem more egalitarian on abstract issues such as increased social status for women or, a more unlikely event, a female presidential candidate. Women hold more egalitarian attitudes toward housework, employment of women, and women congressional candidates (Losh-Hesselbart, 1987).

In contrast to the flexibility and changes that have been observed in gender-role attitudes over the past several years, gender stereotypes have remained relatively stable. Despite the alteration in attitudes and in female employment and increases in two-job families, selected attributes (e.g., intelligence, leadership ability, personality characteristics) continue to be more highly valued and/or seen as more desirable for one sex than for the other. These stereotypes extend to relationships between spouses. Gerber (1987), for example, observed that the stereotypic conception of marriage was one in which more traits that were socially desirable and that reflected power were attributed to the husband. Losh-Hesselbart (1987) posited that the limited changes in income differentials, occupational gender segregation, and responsibility for housework may be related to the continuing pervasive gender stereotyping.

In this book gender-role attitudes subscribed to by husbands, wives, and single persons are included in examinations of well-being. A number of questions were explored: Were men who practiced nontraditional gender roles disadvantaged relative to mental health and work-family role strain? Were married and single-parent employed mothers advantaged or disadvantaged by traditional gender-role attitudes? How did spouses' gender-role attitudes affect the well-being of the other? Were older persons who expressed less traditional gender-role attitudes and engaged in less gender-linked behavior likely to enjoy better mental health?

Clearly, modification of traditional gender-role attitudes may have implications for work-family relationships and for the division of labor internal to the family. Gender-role attitudes are included in analyses of masculine and feminine activities in the family to assess their effects, if any, on the division of labor. All of these questions and issues were considered in the context of available knowledge about the life course and family life stages.

THOUGHTS ABOUT LIFE STAGES

To explore linkages between relationships and well-being, this book focuses on adulthood. Students of life-span developmental psychology remind us that adulthood is a time marked by continuing change, in-

cluding a series of transitions from one situation to another, each requiring the performance of distinct tasks involving new behaviors and
attitudes. The study of adulthood has not always been conceived of in
this way.

Following the rapid changes of adolescence, adulthood was thought
by scholars to be characterized by a sameness that remained virtually
unaltered until old age. Given such a static view of adulthood, it is
perhaps not surprising that this stage of life has been underrepresented
in empirical investigations (Fry, 1983). More recent conceptualizations
of adulthood by both psychologists and sociologists emphasize it as a
dynamic time of life embracing change and variation. In considering
adulthood and the range of ages it encompasses, we employ the concepts
of family life cycle stages and the life course. Following other scholars,
we refer to the life cycle of the family (Mattessich & Hill, 1987; Rexroat
& Shehan, 1987) and to the life course of individuals. We use the terms
"family life cycle" and "family life stages" interchangeably.

The concept of the family cycle, family life cycle, or somewhat less
frequently identified as the "family career," encompasses the family unit
from its beginning to its dissolution (Aldous, 1978). Time periods
through which families pass are viewed as stages. "A stage is a division
within the lifetime of a family that is distinctive enough from those that
precede and follow it to constitute a separate period" (Aldous, 1978:80).
The concept of stage presupposes qualitative changes that are clearly
discernible in such a way that earlier interaction patterns are distin-
guishable from those that occur later. Particular stages span sizeable
amounts of time. Even though stages may blur into one another, dis-
continuities between them differentiate activities within them. The dis-
continuities result in changes in the organization of the family or of the
individual.

Developmental theorists conceptualize the family as a dynamic system
and by doing so call our attention to the interrelationships of family
members in different stages of the life course. Role demands differ by
family life stages, and expectations for behavior change with transitions
from one stage to another. It is thought that families in similar stages
confront comparable difficulties and benefits that differ from those of
previous or later stages. Demands that accompany entry into new stages
require different patterns of family interaction to address them. Furthermore, "There are similarities in the content of the roles and role
clusters of members of families in the same stages" (Aldous, 1978:80).
But as individual families move from one stage to another, the role
clusters change. The concept of family life cycle stages provides an index
of the allocation of roles within the family (Mattessich & Hill, 1987). The
use of stages is based on the assumption that modal patterns of development are experienced by families, even though each individual family

will manifest idiosyncratic features (Mattessich & Hill, 1987). Families in the same stage will be addressing similar developmental tasks.

The concepts of life course and family life cycle stages are useful because they alert us to variation in needs, behavior, privileges, and responsibilities over time in the lives of persons as individuals, as spouses, and as members of families. Unlike an individual, a family is not an organism; its maintenance is dependent on members performing a variety of tasks and remaining in the group. Family members interact and are interdependent, and their behavior is responsive to the expectations of others in the unit (Aldous, 1978). In studies of life stages, then, the reciprocal nature of adjustments among family members is highlighted (Cunningham & Antill, 1984).

The process is a dynamic one, as families identify and devise new means of approaching emergent demands before they routinize patterns to be maintained on a more permanent basis. With transitions required by new roles, families repeat the process in which demands are recognized, alternative ways of addressing them are considered, and finally more routine mechanisms are developed to manage them.

For the scholar, the usefulness of the concept of stages is, in part, derived from the occurrence of similar activities, joys, and problems confronted by families in the same stage. Both the activities and the barriers to carrying them out are shared by families in similar stages. Therefore, there is comparability in the roles as well as in the role strains of families in the same stages. Studies of the life course emphasize regularities in a series of recurring events (Cunningham & Antill, 1984).

A central focus of this book is on life stages as they relate to various aspects of work-family relationships, outlooks on life, and thoughts about gender roles and work. The notions of life course and family life stages usually must include some attention to chronological age of individuals or family members, but other less-clear markers are inextricably imbedded in the concepts as well. There is some debate about the relevance of chronological age for development, with some claiming that it is unimportant and others viewing it as intrinsic to understanding the process of development. Most methods for identifying family life cycle stages employ the age of children as at least one indicator to demarcate and operationalize the stages (Mattessich & Hill, 1987). Chronological age also is thought to be important in relation to developmental tasks.

Therefore, operationalization of stages of the family life cycle take into account the aging of the partners and of their children. For wives, the family life cycle reflects the changing salience of their function as caregivers to children and, for some, the nature of their employment outside the home. For men, and increasingly for women, the intensity of occupational involvement may vary in response to demands associated with place in the family life cycle. The type of involvement in the household by husbands and wives also changes over the life course (Rexroat & Shehan, 1987). In attempting to understand how activities and relationships of spouses and families change over time, a family-development approach takes into account the age of husbands and wives, the presence or absence of children, the age of children, employment outside the home, retirement, and involvement in the household and how these factors influence allocation of time. In this book we observe how some of these aspects of family life impact well-being.

Aldous (1978:83) observed that the primary focus of family-development analysis has centered "on significant changes in the internal organization of married couples who at some time in their marriages are engaged in bearing and rearing children." Consequently, many of the stages delineated and operationalized in research on the family life cycle have as their points of transition events that involve children, that is, their birth, their entrance into and progression through formal education, the youngest child's departure from home, and the remaining aging parents. As might be anticipated, the number of and criteria for stages vary somewhat, depending on the research interest (Menaghan, 1983). Aldous, for example, identified seven stages, beginning with the newly established couple and concluding with aging families, whereas Menaghan in a longitudinal study of marital stress and family transitions specified ten transitional and four stable groups, ranging from new parents as a transitional group to the empty nest, representing a stable group. As is noted in chapter 2, the information in this book is based on families in four life-cycle stages: (1) young families with young children (wife less than 45 years of age and at least one child under six years), (2) maturing families with children in school (at least one child aged six to 18 years), (3) middle-aged empty-nest families (wife aged 45 years or over, no children in the home), and (4) older families (wife aged 60 years or over, no children in the home).

The family-development perspective may be used by scholars as a framework in which to view correlates of stages of the family life cycle. Or a central task may be to describe or explain the phenomenon of family development itself rather than treating it as a determinant of other processes within the family (Mattessich & Hill, 1987). Neither family-development nor life-course analysis are theories (Aldous, 1990). Rather, "Both approaches indicate 'types of variables' that the researcher needs to consider but do not specify 'determinate relationships' among particular variables" (Aldous, 1990:571).

In the chapters that follow, however, family life stages are studied as correlates of processes within the families and as factors that may relate to well-being. Family life stages have been investigated in relation to numerous indices of well-being, including marital satisfaction, parental satisfaction, equity in marital roles, mental health, and general life satisfaction (Mattessich & Hill, 1987). In this research we consider the concept of family life stage only for the married couples because the single-parent families were not selected on the basis of factors that demarcate stages. Even so, single-parent families are thought to need to accomplish developmental tasks at fairly uniform times in their life stages although these stages may not be identical to those for intact families (Mattessich & Hill, 1987).

Well-Being

More generally, measures of well-being may be viewed as social indicators of quality of life. Both objective and subjective indicators of quality of life have been identified. Perceptions of well-being, which are subjective, are one type of indicator of quality of life (Campbell, Converse, & Rodgers, 1976; Keith, 1985a). Promotion of the well-being of individuals is a primary goal of most modern societies, although there is variation in what is thought to constitute well-being and how it is attained.

There are a number of approaches to research on perceptions of well-being (Campbell et al., 1976). One approach is to investigate component parts of well-being; another tack, the one used here, is to identify factors that influence well-being. We consider how individuals assess aspects of their family life, finances, and work and observe how these evaluations affect well-being. Specifically, a major focus is on work and family-role relationships and how evaluations of these relationships (e.g., equitable/inequitable, satisfying/dissatisfying) influence psychological well-being. Evaluations of roles include assessments of equity/inequity, agreement/disagreement between spouses, satisfaction/dissatisfaction, competent/incompetent performance of work-family roles, and the perception of relative deprivation in work-family roles. Self-concept, role strain, and depression are among the primary indicators of well-being. In subsequent chapters, indices of subjective well-being and their correlates are investigated in relation to the family life stage of married couples and for subgroups such as one- and two-job families, modern and traditional families, and single parents and by gender.

2

Methodology

THE LIFE-STAGE GROUPS

The life-stage groups selected for investigation reflect major demarcations in the family life cycle. Group 1 includes young families with preschool children in the home. Group 2 represents maturing families with school-age children. Middle-aged empty-nest families in which children have left the home comprise Group 3, and elderly couples form Group 4. These types of households were adapted from a study by Cross, Herrmann, and Warland (1975) and represent a variety of living arrangements; they are not inclusive of all styles. The criteria used in the definition of the four groups were major role transitions that are inextricably linked with age and that reflect family life stages. The four life stages are introduced by critical changes in role expectations or in actual role performance of spouses and their families: being a parent to young children, having children in school, seeing mature children leave home and set up their own families, and finally confronting the retirement of one or both spouses. In addition to the families in the four life stages, an additional group is included in the study: single–female-parent households. This latter group reflects recent social trends identified in chapter 1 that have implications for family structure.

THE SAMPLE

The universe for the sample that provided information for this book consisted of all households in incorporated towns and cities in Iowa located in one of five life stages defined as follows:

Group 1. Two-parent households containing at least one child less than 6 years old and in which the wife was less than 45 years old

Group 2. Two-parent households containing no child less than 6 years old but at least one child between 6 and 18 years old

Group 3. Married-couple households containing no children and in which the wife was between 45 and 59 years of age

Group 4. Married-couple households containing no children and in which the wife was 60 years or older

Group 5. Single-parent households containing at least one child less than 19 years old

Because one goal of the investigation was to examine the correlates of well-being in different life-styles, this analysis was based on the characteristics of the five types of households separately rather than on composite estimates for the combined groups. For this purpose, with no information about variation among households within groups to indicate otherwise, selections of roughly equal sample sizes in the five groups was determined to be the best procedure to follow.

Because data were to be collected by personal interview, it was possible to use an area sample. A distinguishing characteristic of an area sample is that the sampling unit is not the individual unit of interest (in this study, a household) but rather a piece of land called an area segment that is expected to contain a group or cluster of units of interest. The probability of having selected a particular piece of land (and the households associated with it) is known. Because all households can be associated with some piece of land, the sample frame always completely covers the universe and is up-to-date.

Because the numbers of households in each group varied, different sampling rates were required in order to obtain equal sample sizes. To achieve these different rates, an overall sampling rate was set that was expected to yield the required number of households in the smallest group (Group 1). All households falling into this group were to be interviewed. Households falling into the other groups were subsampled in a systematic manner as they were identified. The subsampling rates

Table 2.1
Selected Background Characteristics of Respondents in Family Life Stages

	Stage I		Stage II		Stage III		Stage IV		Single-Parent Female
	Husband	Wife	Husband	Wife	Husband	Wife	Husband	Wife	
Number of respondents	85	85	88	88	81	81	82	82	78
Age ($\bar{X}$)	30	28	42	40	56	54	71	69	35
Years married ($\bar{X}$)	6.9	6.9	19	19	30	30	43	43	
Number of children in the home	1.95	1.95	2.08	2.08					2.07

were determined so as to yield the desired number of households in each group.

The sample was stratified to include metropolitan areas, cities with populations between 10,000 and 49,999, and smaller communities under 10,000. Thus, the sample can be described as a stratified, multistage, self-weighting area sample. Households were subsampled at constant rates; therefore, equal overall probabilities were maintained within groups. Having equal probabilities enables one to estimate population means and proportions directly from the corresponding simple sample means and proportions without having to apply any weights to the data.

A total of 541 households were contacted (90 single-parent females, 113 stage 1 couples, 121 stage 2 couples, 102 stage 3 couples, and 115 stage 4 couples). Of the total sample of 992 persons 14.7 percent refused to be interviewed and 3.9 percent were not interviewed because of illness or inability to locate and in 5.8 percent of the couple households only one spouse was interviewed. Households in the last situation were excluded from the sample. Therefore, the acceptance rate was 75.6 percent, resulting in 750 subjects (336 couples/672 subjects and 78 single-parent females). Table 2.1 arranges the sample groups by life-cycle stage, shows the number of interviews completed in each group, and also reports the average values of selected background characteristics of the sample.

INTERVIEW PROCEDURES

The interview schedule was constructed to measure patterns of interpersonal and family relationships and well-being. It was pretested on individuals similar to those represented by the five life-stage groups. The interview was administered in the home of the respondents by trained interviewers. Twenty-three interviewers were hired and received extensive training in screening procedures and the administration of the questionnaire. Once it was determined a household would fit one of the life stages specified, the person contacted would be interviewed or a call-back appointment made. In the case of married couples, an appointment was often made to return and interview the spouse at a later date. Married couples were interviewed separately. The interview took approximately one hour to complete.

MEASURES

Work-Family Roles

A set of measures was developed to assess well-being. Specific measures focused on the individual and addressed psychological distress (e.g., self-concept and depressive symptoms); others examined tension in relationships. For this investigation, five roles integral to the functioning of the family unit were chosen as the subject for the examination of well-being in marital relationships. Frequently performed roles necessary to the daily maintenance of the family presumably will be salient to marital partners, making it possible to elicit the quality of the marital interaction. Inclusion of a variety of roles provided an opportunity to assess situations requiring different types of skills and activities within and outside the household. Two of the roles selected focused upon the household tasks of cooking and housekeeping. Two others centered upon the interpersonal skills of companionship to the spouse and caring for children (parent). Finally, the provider role was included. This role involves the establishment of ties and interaction with individuals and organizations outside the immediate family. Partners' performance in these roles, and their assessments of them, comprised some of the indicators of well-being.

Dissatisfaction

Role dissatisfaction was determined by asking the respondents how much satisfaction or dissatisfaction they received from "cooking, housekeeping, being a provider, being a companion to their spouse, and caring for and training children (if there were children in the home)." For each of these roles or activities the respondents were given four possible response categories: 1 = "great deal of satisfaction," 2 = "some satisfaction," 3 = "some dissatisfaction," and 4 = "a great deal of dissatisfaction." Role dissatisfaction measures were determined by summing the responses for each of the five roles (or each of the four roles if there were no children at home). A higher score indicated greater role dissatisfaction. The coefficient of reliability for role dissatisfaction was $r = .42$ (alpha).

Disagreement

Role disagreement was determined by asking how often the husbands and wives disagreed about activities in the five different marital roles. For each role the respondents could answer 1 = "never," 2 = "seldom," 3 = "sometimes," 4 = "frequently," and 5 = "always." Responses for each measure were summed to produce a role disagreement score. The coefficient of reliability was r = .68 (alpha).

Role Performance

The respondents' evaluation of their own and their spouses' role performance was determined by asking each partner how well he or she thought he or she performed in the five different activities. Respondents also were asked to rate their spouses' performance in the five activities. They were given a five-point scale to evaluate their own and their spouses' performance with 1 = "much below average" and 5 = "much above average." The reliability coefficient for evaluation of their own role performance was .67 (alpha), and it was .76 (alpha) for their evaluation of their spouses' role performance. The responses for each role were summed to produce measures of self and spousal role performance.

Equity and Inequity

Two measures were used to determine equity in the marital relationship. The first was the Hatfield (1978) Global Measure of Equity/Inequity, which was used to measure the overall assessment of equity. Respondents were asked, "Considering what you put into and get out of your marriage compared to what your partner puts into and gets out of it, how does your marriage relationship stack up?"

1. My partner is getting a much better deal.
2. My partner is getting a somewhat better deal.
3. My partner is getting a slightly better deal.
4. We are both getting an equal deal.
5. I am getting a slightly better deal.
6. I am getting a somewhat better deal.
7. I am getting a much better deal.

The data were coded to reflect a linear trend from inequity to equity. Respondents who experienced greater inequity, being either overbenefited or underbenefited (categories 1 and 7), were combined and assigned the score of 1. Those perceiving less inequity (categories 2 and 6 and categories 3 and 5) were respectively combined and assigned progressively higher scores; those perceiving equity were assigned the highest score. The result was a four-point scale with scores of 1 to 3 equalling high to low inequity and 4 equalling equity.

The second measure of equity/inequity examined the partners' perception of fairness in the performance of selected marital roles. Husbands and wives evaluated their own and their spouses' level of effort in the five different marital roles. Respondents were first asked about their own performance. "Do you feel you should either increase or decrease your own efforts in the following tasks to make the marriage relationship more fair for both of you?" The respondents were asked to select one of five possible answers: 1 = "decrease effort a great deal," 2 = "decrease effort somewhat," 3 = "present effort is fair," 4 = "increase effort somewhat," or 5 = "increase effort a great deal."

To measure perceptions of their spouses' level of effort in the marital roles, respondents were asked, "Do you feel your husband/wife should either increase or decrease his/her efforts in the following tasks to make the marriage relationship more fair for both of you?" The same five choices were used again, with responses to these questions coded from 1 for "decrease effort a great deal" to 5 for "increase effort a great deal." The equity score for each respondent was determined by taking the difference in scores of self-evaluation and evaluation of spouse on each of the five roles. Subtracting the evaluation of spouses' efforts from the respondents' evaluation of their own efforts resulted in a nine-point scale, ranging from -4 to $+4$. Inequity that was unfavorable to the respondent was represented by scores of -1 to -4. Respondents within this classification were underbenefited. They felt that their spouses' efforts were less adequate than their own and that either they had to decrease their efforts or their spouses needed to increase their efforts. Zero on the -4 to $+4$ scale represented equity, in which the respondents perceived a balance between their own and their spouses' efforts in marital roles. Scores of 1 to 4 represented perceived inequity that was favorable to the respondent. Respondents in this classification were overbenefited. They felt that their own efforts were less adequate than their spouses' and that either they had to increase their own efforts or their spouses needed to decrease their efforts.

Depressive Symptoms

A scale developed by Derogatis, Lipman, Covi, and Rickles (1971) and used elsewhere (Pearlin, 1975; Pearlin & Johnson, 1977) was selected as an indicator of psychological distress. Respondents were asked to indicate the frequency (1 = "never" to 5 = "very often") with which they experienced the following symptoms: "lack enthusiasm for doing anything, have a poor appetite, feel bored or have little interest in things, lose sexual interest or pleasure, have trouble getting to sleep or staying asleep, cry easily or feel like crying, feel down-hearted or blue, feel low in energy or slowed down, feel hopeless about the future, have any thoughts of possibly ending your life, feel lonely." Data were coded so that a high score reflected greater depressive symptoms. The coefficient of reliability for the eleven items was .79 (alpha).

Role Strain

Work-family role strain was measured by the frequency (1 = "never" to 5 = "very often") with which respondents felt bothered by four situations: feeling that their job outside the home may interfere with their family life, feeling that family life may interfere with the job outside the home, thinking that the amount of work they have to do may interfere with how well it gets done, and feeling that others in the family will not do household tasks as well as they would do them. Data were coded so that a high score indicated higher work-family strain (.65, alpha).

Attitudes toward Gender Roles

Two measures of attitudes toward gender roles were developed. Attitudes toward women's roles were measured by agreement/disagreement with three items: "Women with young children should not work outside the home"; "For a woman, marriage and family should be more important than work and a career"; "All in all, the emotional life of a family suffers when a woman has a full-time job or career." Response categories ranged from 1 = "strongly agree" to 5 = "strongly disagree." Responses were summed so that a higher score indicated more traditional attitudes. The coefficient of reliability was .73 (alpha).

Orientations toward work-family tasks were assessed by asking who respondents thought should have responsibility for four activities: earning the family income, cooking, housekeeping (except cooking and child care), and caring for and training children. Responses, which ranged from 1 = "husband always" to 5 = "wife always," were coded and summed so that a higher score reflected more nontraditional beliefs. The coefficient of reliability was .62 (alpha).

Work Commitment

Work commitment was assessed by responses to the following four questions: "If I inherited so much money that I did not have to work,

I would still work"; "I enjoy my spare-time activities much more than my work"; "My work is more satisfying to me than the time I spend around the house"; "To me, my work is just a way of making money." Responses ranged from 1 to 5, with 1 = "strongly disagree," and 5 = "strongly agree." Data were coded so that a higher score reflected a greater commitment to work.

Comparisons of Family Type, Work, and Finances

To obtain comparative evaluations of one- and two-job families, women compared their general life situation with that of women who were full-time homemakers. Response categories ranged from 1 = "much worse off" to 5 = "much better off." Using the same response categories, men in two-job families compared their situation with that of men whose wives were full-time homemakers. Respondents compared their work and financial situations with others of the same age and sex using categories ranging from 1 = "much worse off" to 5 = "much better off."

Involvement in Masculine and Feminine Tasks

Involvement in masculine tasks was assessed by asking respondents which spouse usually did yard work and household repairs with responses ranging from 1 = "spouse always" to 5 = "self always" with 3 = "husband and wife about the same." The items were summed with a higher score reflecting greater involvement in masculine tasks in the household.

Following Ross, Mirowsky, and Huber (1983), one measure of feminine activities asked respondents who usually did the cooking and housekeeping. Response categories were from 1 = "husband always" to 5 = "wife always." The items were summed with a higher score representing a more traditional allocation of housework between spouses.

A second measure of participation in feminine tasks included the frequency with which husbands and wives were involved with laundry, grocery shopping, and dishwashing (1 = "spouse always does" to 5 = "self does most"). These three items were summed so that a higher score indicated greater involvement in the tasks.

These measures are the most frequently used in the chapters that follow. Other measures are described in the chapters in which they are used. For example, construction of the typologies (i.e., marital role congruence and marriage types) are detailed in chapter 6. Measures of self-concept are presented in chapter 7.

3

Work and Well-Being in One- and Two-Job Families

This chapter has three objectives: (1) to describe how these single- and dual-earner families were similar and different in the ways in which work-related factors impinged on their lives, (2) to consider selected employment and work characteristics in relation to the work-family strain of men and women, and (3) to investigate the influence of objective and subjective characteristics of employment and finances on depressive symptoms.

Several themes in popular and social science literature either directly or by implication focus on problems that occur when men and women try to allocate time between work and family. Sometimes research has dealt with only the consequences of the employment of husbands, or sometimes that of wives, but labor-force involvement often has been investigated from the standpoint of difficulties rather than of benefits. Depending on when the research was conducted, employed husbands and wives have variously been profiled as villains, especially if they were viewed as neglecting their families, or as victims of role overload. Earlier literature on the consequences of the employment of both husbands and wives generally tended to emphasize deficits that work may create for the individual, the family, or the marital relationship (Burke, Weir & DuWors, 1980; Keith & Schafer, 1983; Spitze, 1988).

Ideally the employment characteristics of both spouses should be examined in relationship to the well-being of the other, but research frequently has considered the impact of only one spouse's characteristics, neglecting the reciprocal nature of the marital relationship (Keith &

Schafer, 1983). Several investigations of well-being in the family have considered the labor-force involvement of the wife alone (employed versus full-time homemaker) as the primary employment variable, with few if any additional work characteristics of either spouse included (e.g., Rosenfield, 1980). Only recently have the work-family demands of both spouses been investigated simultaneously, and researchers have been admonished about the need to examine parallel consequences of men's and women's employment and the joint outcomes of their work for families (Spitze, 1988).

In some of the earlier anecdotal literature, involvement of men in work was reflected in the somewhat stereotypic profile of the husband so intensely committed to work that his family suffered from his psychological and physical absence and emotional neglect (Seidenberg, 1973). In this type of research, the impact of the husband's work behavior on the family was scrutinized. As women moved into the labor force, investigation of the influence of female employment on the family initially centered on the effect of maternal employment on children (e.g., Hoffman & Nye, 1975); but more recently, although to a lesser degree, it has focused on the implications of wives' work outside the home for their husbands' welfare (Kessler & McRae, 1982; Mortimer, 1980; Pleck, 1985). Thus, at various periods of time both husbands and wives have been viewed as potentially disadvantaged by the other's employment. Spitze (1988) suggested that the consequences of female employment have been treated like the outcomes of unemployment for men. Even though a prevailing popular conclusion has been that female employment, especially, holds few benefits for either children or spouses, research has failed to demonstrate predominantly negative effects.

Role difficulties in the workplace and at home and the interface between them have been found to be stressors that, in turn, may have deleterious physical and psychological outcomes (Lewis & Cooper, 1987). With some exceptions, researchers have long viewed multiple role occupancy in terms of its negative effects. Generally, diversified roles have been conceptualized as leading to role strain and subsequently to harmful consequences for individual well-being. The thinking has been that multiple roles will have the potential for conflicting expectations or multiple demands that exceed the time and energy of the individual (Thoits, 1987). Conflicting expectations and multiple demands are two of the possible outcomes of performing several roles. Theorizing about conflicting expectations has employed the concept of role conflict, and investigation of the consequences of multiple demands has used the concept of role strain. Role conflict may occur when there are conflicting demands within and between roles, whereas strain refers to the felt difficulty in performing a role and may encompass overload and ambiguity. But the concepts of strain and conflict have been defined and operationalized in various ways (Voydanoff, 1988). Work-family role strain is used here to denote difficulty in performing role obligations, and it is important to our analysis of the interface between work and family.

However they are defined, conflict and strain as consequences of multiple roles sometimes have prompted the conclusion that holding more roles fosters psychological distress and perhaps physical difficulties. A common assumption related to work-family activities is that role strain, for example, may follow from women's employment and men's parenting and homemaking tasks because of their interference with the demands of traditional activities (Lewis & Cooper, 1987). In our research, work-family strain implied that demands of the workplace and of the home were in some way incompatible, so that involvement in either was more difficult because of participation in the other (Voydanoff, 1988).

THE OTHER SIDE OF ROLE OVERLOAD

For some scholars, focusing on the injurious aspects of multiple roles has obscured the possibility that with variety and diversity also may come privileges and advantages not otherwise available. Role strain theory highlights the potentially adverse aspects of diversity at the expense of not taking into account the rewards. Sieber (1974) and others, however, have observed that it is the very accumulated roles with their potential disadvantages that may provide the flexibility to manage multiple demands. Obligations accompanying one role may be used to address demands occurring in another. The adult student, for example, may employ the demands of other role obligations to justify poor performance in or neglect of academic work. Conversely, pressures of academic demands may be used to justify slighting obligations to family or employers. Diversified roles may enhance status and provide privileges that facilitate role performances. Furthermore, personality enrichment and ego gratification may follow from multiple roles, despite their sometimes conflicting demands (Sieber, 1974). Recently Thoits (1987) has posited how multiple roles may foster a set of social identities for persons that may increase their sense of purpose and diminish feelings of anxiety and despair.

In addition to the two perspectives that emphasize either the advantages or the disadvantages of multiple roles, a third theme in the literature attends to the quality of experiences in various aspects of life rather than attempting to speculate about the hazards or benefits of role accumulation. This perspective addresses the question, "How do roles in which people are involved and the nature of their experiences in them affect their well-being?" Although these queries have been directed most often to women, they are equally germane to the lives of men. Furthermore, not only may men and women have disparate experiences in similar roles, but these roles also may have differential effects on their well-being.

In representative research on women only, Baruch and Barnett (1987) investigated self-esteem, depression, and pleasure in relation to the number of their roles along with the quality of their experiences as workers, wives, and mothers. They confirmed the relationship between the quality of role experiences and well-being and observed that mere occupancy of a role, independent of the response to it, did not enhance well-being. They concluded that because role occupancy fails to predict well-being with much consistency, it is no longer useful to debate simply whether a larger or smaller number of roles is optimal for adjustment and a satisfactory quality of life (Baruch & Barnett, 1987).

Others, however, have found that benefits may be derived from diversity (Gove & Zeiss, 1987). In general, gender differentiates the number and types of roles held and perhaps some of the perquisites obtained from involvement. For example, men occupy more roles than women and experience more advantages in marriage, although marital quality seems of greater importance to the overall well-being of women (Gove & Zeiss, 1987). In addition to marital experiences, the meaning of employment and parental roles and their implications for happiness also are somewhat gender-linked. As a whole, though, occupying multiple roles seems beneficial for both men and women, and the quality of experiences in given roles is salient to well-being, as is the amount of diversity.

Although research on two-job families more often has investigated employment and nonemployment in relation to well-being, specific characteristics of work also have been linked to the physical and mental health of individuals (Mortimer, Lorence, & Kumka, 1986; O'Toole, 1975). In previous research, for example, the relationship between employment characteristics such as occupational level, job satisfaction, type of pressures at work, work time, occupational involvement, and mental health and well-being have been studied (Burke et al., 1980; Mortimer, 1980; Mortimer et al., 1986; O'Toole, 1975). Spitze (1988) called attention to the need to focus on the consequences of characteristics of employment rather than differences by employment status alone. Voydanoff (1988) followed this admonition by assessing the following characteristics of work: amount and scheduling of work time, job demands including workload pressure, work-role conflict and ambiguity, and enriching job demands. In this chapter, the characteristics of work that affected the work-family strain of dual-earner couples and that of men in single-earner households were investigated and the importance of both subjective and objective aspects of employment for work-family strain were assessed.

THEORETICAL CONSIDERATIONS: SUBJECTIVE EVALUATIONS, SOCIAL COMPARISONS, AND WELL-BEING

Social-psychological theory and research have posited and supported the assumption that subjective evaluations of different domains influence the total quality of life experiences (Campbell et al., 1976; Keith, 1985a). Objective characteristics explain incompletely the perceptions of various facets of life. Attitudes and values may intervene between objective personal attributes and subsequent evaluations of situations (Keith & Lorenz, 1989). Indeed, subjective evaluations of areas of life such as work or family may be more salient in determining attitudes or other dimensions of behavior than are objective characteristics (e.g., income, occupational status, time spent at work, or number of responsibilities). Sometimes subjective assessments of circumstances are at variance with objective indices and fail to show a positive change even when improvement in a situation or status has occurred (Keith & Lorenz, 1989).

Theorizing about the importance of subjective evaluations to mental health may be extended to include processes of social comparison. Social-psychological theory indicates that individuals evaluate the adequacy of relationships or situations relative to those experienced by others (Thibaut & Kelley, 1959). Persons are believed to have standards against which they gauge the acceptability of the outcomes they obtain from a relationship or situation. Perceptions of deprivation or advantage, for example, may be derived from comparisons with generalized others. Crosby (1982) identified a number of cognitions and emotions that may be psychological preconditions for feelings of deprivation or benefit. These include wanting, entitlement, comparisons with others, and past and future expectations. General comparisons reveal how individuals assess their own situation in a larger matrix (Crosby, 1982). In turn, general social comparisons may be important in determining consequences that individuals believe they deserve based on their efforts in specific relationships or situations. Theory suggests that clear linkages will be observed between persons' evaluations of a variety of aspects of their lives and psychological well-being. It was anticipated that the well-being of the employed in both one- and two-job families would be associated with comparative appraisals of the employment characteristics of their partners. For example, individuals in single-earner families may want and believe that they deserve both spouses to be employed, whereas only one partner in the two-job family may prefer to work outside the home but both must contribute to the family income. These feelings of deprivation or benefit derived from general comparisons with others may figure in psychological well-being.

Strain and Subjective Characteristics of One- and Two-Job Families

On the assumption that subjective dimensions were important in evaluating various aspects of life and that conclusions drawn from social comparisons figured in well-being, two types of subjective factors were examined. One group of subjective dimensions included attitudes toward work and values assigned to work (e.g., job satisfaction, work orientation) and performance as an earner (e.g., evaluation of self/spouse in the provider role). It was expected that both lower job satisfaction and negative evaluations of performance in the provider role would be associated with diminished psychological well-being.

A second type of subjective factors involved comparative evaluations of work and financial circumstances vis-à-vis the fortunes of others and reflections about the relative benefit or disadvantage of life in dual-versus single-earner households. Because work is believed to be a salient life area for many men and perhaps increasingly for women, to the degree that work, financial situation, and involvement in a particular family pattern (i.e., dual- versus single-earner) were found to be unattractive compared to the circumstances of others, they were anticipated to have a negative effect on mental health and be conducive to strain. Furthermore, it was expected that comparative evaluations of work and family situations would have an independent effect on well-being when aspects of employment such as job satisfaction and commitment to work were considered. Consonance between their preferences and what families are able to attain will likely foster appreciative comparisons, less strain, and better psychological health.

Strain and Objective Employment Characteristics in One- and Two-Job Families

Both the subjective assessments of work-family factors just noted and objective characteristics of employment may foster strain. A number of objective dimensions of work-family situations have been considered in relation to strain by scholars (Lewis & Cooper, 1987; Voydanoff, 1988). One group of these factors is associated with time demands. A major dimension of employment is the amount of time that persons spend on the job. The amount of time spent at work is reflected not only in earnings and benefits but perhaps also in overload, if the amount is excessive relative to other claims on the time of the individual. Extensive time spent in employment usually restricts the amount of time workers are physically available to family members, and employment that takes place at less traditional times also interferes with family activities (Voydanoff, 1988). Thus, not only does time spent in employment affect the efforts of the worker but also, in a reciprocal relationship such as marriage, the activities of one partner shape those of the other.

Overload can be thought of as multiple demands that exceed resources (Lewis & Cooper, 1987). Time is a primary resource and an integral aspect of measures of overload. Earlier research on role strain considered the implications that the number of hours that persons spent at work per week hold for stress. That is, what are the consequences of spending more time at work in terms of both the strain on and well-being of the individual and its effect on the spouse? Much research has found a positive relationship between the number of hours persons work and their work-family strain and conflict (Voydanoff, 1988). But the outcomes may differ for husbands and wives. For example, the number of hours that their husbands worked was a factor in the strain of wives, but the time spent at work by women did not foster strain among their partners (Keith & Schafer, 1980).

In this chapter, the claims on the time of spouses both within and outside the household were taken into account. As noted in the chapter on gender roles, theories explaining the division of labor in the household usually take into consideration the time available to both spouses, but the employment status of the wife is especially factored into any explanation. In our research respondents provided estimates of whether they or their spouses spent more time on household tasks typically viewed as masculine or feminine (e.g., maintenance or housework). Thus, allocation of time pertained to both work and family activities. Other objective indices included in the models of strain were demographic characteristics: age, family income, occupational level, and number of children in the home.

Another set of factors comprised the subjective aspects of work and finances. Subjective indicators that were used were of two types: (1) evaluations by individuals of their lives compared with those of their age and sex peers in areas of work, finances, and family structure (i.e., an evaluation of a dual- versus single-earner family type) and (2) work-related indices including an assessment of performance in the provider role by self and by spouse, satisfaction with their own performance, job satisfaction, and commitment to work. These objective and subjective dimensions were studied in relation to strain among employed men and women in single- and dual-earner families. Models of strain are estimated for employed women and men, but not for homemakers, who did not respond to the same questions. The relative effects of time demands of work both inside and outside the home as well as the perceived quality of experiences and objective characteristics on the role strain of employed persons in two different family patterns were assessed.

RESULTS

Work-Family Strain

How were workers in these one- and two-job families differentially affected by work-family role strain? First, men in one- and two-job households did not differ in the amount of work-family strain they reported ($\overline{X}$ = 1.96, 2.04) although women in dual-earner families were more strained ($\overline{X}$ = 2.31) than either group of men. For earlier scholars, the concern was that family obligations would interfere with work, but the workers we studied were more likely to anticipate that their jobs at some time might interfere with their family life (69 and 77 percent of men and women, respectively) rather than that family activities would conflict with their jobs (49 and 55 percent of men and women, respectively). Overload was prevalent; about 76 percent of the employed men and 87 percent of the women at some time felt burdened that the amount of work they had to do interfered with how well they were able to do it. Feeling that others in the family would not do household tasks as well was substantially more troublesome for women than for men, probably indicating their greater responsibility for managing these activities; only 16 percent of employed women never worried about this situation compared to 48 percent of the men.

Employment Characteristics of Men in One- and Two-Job Families

Did men in one- and two-job families differ in employment characteristics? As a whole, the work characteristics of the men were fairly comparable. Time demands of employment were similar, with both working an average of forty-seven to forty-eight hours per week, although men in one-job families tended to be employed in slightly lower-ranked occupations than their counterparts in dual-earner families (t = 1.77, $p < .10$). Probably because husbands' occupational placement was lower and because their spouses were not employed, total income in one-job families was somewhat less (t = 2.35, $p < .05$). Men in one- and two-job families did not differ in work commitment or the belief that their work situation compared favorably with that of others, and they assessed their earning capacities comparably. On two dimensions, however, men in single-earner families tended to be somewhat more advantaged: they felt less deprived by their overall financial circumstances ($t = 1.80$, $p < .10$), and they tended to find greater satisfaction in their jobs ($t = 1.70$, $p < .10$). Despite having less income they viewed their financial situation more favorably, and although they worked in somewhat lower-status occupations, they enjoyed greater job satisfaction. The differences, however, were quite small. Even though we assume that some aspects of the lives of men will vary depending on employment patterns in the family, selected work experiences of these men were quite similar.

Employment Characteristics of Husbands and Wives

To what extent did husbands and wives share similar employment characteristics and perspectives on work? The answer to these questions may provide some insight into the context in which dual-earner families articulated their work and family responsibilities.

Husbands spent considerably more time at work, forty-eight hours per week compared to their wives' thirty hours per week ($t = 11.43$, $p < .001$, paired t). Correspondingly, husbands indicated a somewhat stronger commitment to work ($t = 1.86$, $p < .10$), and they evaluated their performance as a provider more positively than did their wives ($t = 7.36$, $p < .001$). Even though they described greater role strain ($t = 4.02$, $p < .001$), wives were as likely as husbands to be satisfied with their jobs ($t = 1.24$, not significant (NS)). Husbands and wives had similar views of the conflict in their relationship ($t = .06$, NS) although corroborating other literature, wives reported more depressive symptoms ($t = 4.66$, $p < .001$). For the most part then, despite their more limited involvement in work, employed wives seemed more stressed than their husbands.

Multivariate Models of Role Strain

Which objective and subjective factors seemed to have the greatest effect on work-family strain? Further, were there common patterns across the three groups of respondents—men in one-job families, employed women, and employed men in dual-earner families? To answer these questions, separate multiple regression analyses of objective and subjective factors and work-family strain were conducted for the three groups (Table 3.1). As noted in chapter 2, work-family strain was assessed by the frequency ("never" to "very often") with which persons felt bothered by feeling that their job outside the home might interfere with family life, feeling that family life might interfere with their job outside the home, thinking that the amount of work they had to do might interfere with how well it was done, and feeling that others in the family might not do household tasks as well as they would. A higher

Table 3.1

Work-Family Strain and Employment Characteristics of Husbands and Wives in One- and Two-Job Families (Multiple Regression Analyses)

	Husbands in One-Job Families N = 130		Husbands in Two-Job Families N = 135		Wives in Two-Job Families N = 135	
	r	Beta	r	Beta	r	Beta
Hours per week	.30	.27**	.47	.34***	.13	.27**
Spouses' strain	.29	.24**	.21	.12	.20	.23*
Age	-.20	-.07	-.16	-.28**	-.14	.10
Income	-.02	-.13	.22	.22*	.10	.08
Work commitment	.18	.26*	.23	.16	.04	-.06
Job satisfaction	.06	-.22	.04	-.18	.17	.26**
Evaluation as earner	.04	.08	-.02	-.24**	.08	.02
Evaluation spouse as earner			-.16	-.22**	00	00
Cross-gender tasks	-.18	-.16	.02	.03	-.19	-.23*
R^2		.30		.43		.22

* p <.10
** p <.05
*** p <.01

score indicated greater strain. In addition to the objective and subjective indicators previously described, one of the models also included spouses' strain. Analyses in which characteristics of spouses' employment were included are reported but are not shown. Because queries about strain from employment experiences were not appropriate for homemakers, only two questions assessing strain were asked of women not employed outside the home—feeling that the amount of work interfered with how well it was done and feeling that others in the household might not do tasks as well as they. Responses to these questions were used in the analysis of their husbands' role strain.

To what extent was the actual time spent at work a primary factor in the lives of the employed? Employed men and women in both types of households found that work and family activities interfered with one another when they spent more hours at work. Work-family strain ensuing from the allocation of more time to work was greatest for men in dual-earner families ($r = .47$), somewhat less among men in one-job families ($r = .30$), and least among employed wives ($r = .13$).

Men in two-job families who spent more time at work also were employed in higher-level occupations ($r = .24$), but they were *not* married to women who also worked long hours ($r = 00$). Men in dual-earner households who were more committed to work than to family or leisure spent more time at work ($r = .26$) but commitment to work was less strongly associated with time spent at work by men in single-earner families ($r = .15$). Men and women highly committed to work, however, were not married to one another ($r = .07$), suggesting that it may be difficult to sustain high levels of commitment to work by spouses in the same relationship.

In other ways as well, factors that fostered strain among men in two-job families differed from those that contributed to strain among men in single-earner families and employed women. For example, involvement in the household by men in two-job families was never a factor in their role strain, whereas women in dual-earner couples and men whose wives were homemakers were more advantaged if their spouses assumed responsibility for the traditional gender-typed tasks. That is, they benefited from a traditional division of labor whereas performance of more cross-gender tasks in the household fostered greater strain. But despite concern that men in dual-earner households may become overloaded by increased homemaking tasks, their stress was independent of arrangements for housework, whereas their male counterparts in one-job families were strained when they assumed responsibility for nontraditional activities. When their spouses' role strain was included in the model for men in one-job families, however, the importance of household tasks diminished. Rather, any effects of performance of household tasks were mediated by wife's strain, which in turn was a significant factor in the work-family stress experienced by men in one-job families but not that of dual-earner men.

The strain expressed by dual-earner men seemed to have different origins from that of their wives or their male counterparts in a different family pattern. For example, feelings about how well they thought they and their spouse earned income and actual income were more troubling to them than to men in one-job families. Disappointment with earnings fostered strain, and men in two-job families who were more distressed tended to feel more deprived in the area of finances. Older men with employed spouses were less troubled than their younger peers, whereas age was not a factor in the strain of males in single-earner families. Men in two-job households also were more disturbed by work-family difficulties if their wives spent greater time in the labor force. Feeling negatively about their capabilities as an earner and having their spouse employed extensively outside the home were especially stressful to husbands in dual-earner families.

Employed women and men in single-earner families whose spouses felt greater strain also were more worried about the interference of their

Table 3.2
Patterns of Strain in Two-Job Families

Patterns of Strain	N	Percentage of Two-Job Families
Husband and wife low	45	33
Husband low and wife high	28	21
Husband high and wife low	28	21
Husband and wife high	34	25

work and family responsibilities ($r = .26$ and $.26, p < .001$, for both). Men in two-job households were not more stressed when their wives were burdened with meshing family and work responsibilities.

Occupational status and commitment to work generally did not directly foster strain. Except for men in one-job families for whom their greater work commitment was associated with elevated strain, occupational status and commitment to work were not important in accounting for strain of either employed men or women. Rather, in most instances, if work commitment had any effect on work-family strain, it tended to be indirect and was mediated through increased time devoted to employment. In summary, somewhat different circumstances contributed to the role strain of husbands and wives in two-job families. Additionally, compared to male peers in single-earner families, men whose wives were employed were especially troubled by their subjective evaluations of aspects of the provider role.

Patterns of Role Strain in Two-Job Families

Hinchcliffe, Hooper, and Roberts (1978) posited that the personality characteristics and subjective experiences of one spouse are inexorably interwoven with those of the other. Therefore, we might expect that life in families in which both spouses are strained would be different from those in which both feel less pressure and relatively little stress. There also is the possible pattern in which one spouse is stressed, viewing work and their private life as intruding on one another, while the other partner may characterize his/her occupational and family demands as harmonious.

Based on the work-family role strain of employed couples, four types of families were delineated (Table 3.2). In one pattern, both partners experienced higher amounts of strain (i.e., strained families) whereas in another type each spouse identified little interference between work and family (i.e., unstrained families). In one-third of the families both spouses reported low strain, whereas in 25 percent both partners experienced high strain. In the two remaining patterns, spouses' responses to strain were such that one of them perceived a high level of interference between work and family whereas the other partner viewed these areas of life as intruding less on one another; this resulted in the mixed patterns. Twenty-one percent were in the mixed pattern in which the husband experienced greater strain and the wife was less stressed. An equal proportion (21 percent) of families included wives with higher strain and less stressed husbands.

To examine the relationship between life stage and patterns of strain, the two younger groups of families were combined, as were the middle-aged and older groups. Patterns of strain were strongly associated with family life stages ($\overline{X}$ = 13.06, 3 df, $p < .01$). The most marked differences were in the polar types, strained versus unstrained families. Forty-five percent of the middle-aged and older families were unstrained, whereas only 26 percent of the younger partners both had low role strain. In contrast, younger spouses were more often in highly strained families, 35 percent, compared to only 8 percent of the older couples. About equal proportions of younger (21 percent) and older families (20 percent) were in patterns in which husbands were unstrained but their wives experienced high strain. In 18 percent of the youngest and 27 percent of the oldest families, husbands reported high strain, but their wives were relatively unstrained.

Discriminant analyses were conducted separately for husbands and wives in dual-earner households to investigate whether their employment characteristics and views of their jobs and financial circumstances were linked with patterns of work-family strain. In these analyses, our interest was in learning whether work-related factors would differentiate between types of families, particularly those in which both partners were either highly strained or households in which each spouse reported little distress. To the extent that employment characteristics would differentiate between the types, it was anticipated that the polar but congruent types would differ the most (i.e., couples in which both partners were highly strained versus those in which both were more relaxed).

Presumably families in which spouses experience greater strain would be differentiated from those partners who have a more equable situation. Conditions that foster strain in both spouses and the fact that each feels pressured by conflicting demands of work and family may create a setting conducive to further stress if action is not undertaken to diminish it. This is in conformity with the views of Hinchcliffe and colleagues who posited that distress in either spouse does not leave the other untouched.

Table 3.3
Discriminant Analyses of Strained and Unstrained Two-Job Families

| | Standardized Discriminant Function Coefficients | |
	Husbands N = 135	Wives N = 135
Income	-.20	.07
Occupation	-.17	-.55
Hours per week	-.44	-.28
Age	.73	.92
Work commitment	-.48	.28
Job satisfaction	.55	.38
Comparative financial situation	.24	-.19
Evaluation as earner	.10	.21
Comparative work situation	-.27	-.16
Deprivation in two-job family	.49	.10
Chi-square	67.80 p <.001	43.61 p <.05
Canonical correlation	.60	.46

Men in Strained and Unstrained Families

What were the work and financial experiences of men in strained and unstrained families? In the discriminant analyses, demographic characteristics (age, income, occupation); time spent at work; work commitment; job satisfaction; comparisons of financial, work, and family situations; and evaluation as an earner were considered in relation to patterns of family strain. Men in dual-earner families in which they and their wives were more strained by interference between work and family were differentiated from those in households in which neither spouse was stressed by the interface between work and family demands (Table 3.3). Husbands in strained families were distinguished from their peers in calmer settings by the amount of time they spent at work, age, commitment to work, job satisfaction, and comparisons of their lives with those of men in one-job families. The profile was one in which men in the most stressed households tended to be heavily involved in work, spending an average of fifty-four hours per week compared with the forty-five hours spent by men in less strained families. If there were workaholics among these men, they were those most often burdened by interference between work and family and married to women who shared their perceptions of the family as highly strained.

Men in strained families were younger ($\bar{X}$ = 36 years) than those in any other pattern, with husbands in unstrained families being the oldest ($\overline{X}$ = 49 years). Men in strained families were more committed to work than peers in less-stressed families, and they felt their lives in a two-earner family held fewer advantages. Work commitment, as assessed here, indicated a tendency to find more satisfaction in work than in family activities, being unwilling to give up work even if it were not a financial necessity to continue employment, enjoying work more than spare-time activities, finding work more satisfying than time spent around the house, and deriving intrinsic satisfaction from work rather than regarding it as just a way of making money. These attitudes reflect activities and behavior that if carried out extensively would likely result in potential interference or overlap of work into the domains of family and leisure. Greater job satisfaction, however, was not realized from high work commitment among men in strained families. Men in strained families with high work commitment were the least satisfied with their jobs. It may be that when high work commitment is combined with the feeling that family and employment interfere with one another and role overload is great, job satisfaction will remain elusive. The pressure likely mitigates potential satisfaction. Furthermore, among men in all other family patterns (i.e., unstrained and mixed patterns) a strong commitment to work was accompanied by greater job satisfaction. In strained families men worked the longest hours, were highly committed to work, and derived the least satisfaction from their jobs. The men who seemingly put the most into their work benefited the least. At least they obtained substantially fewer intrinsic benefits.

Several work characteristics of these husbands then differentiated strained and unstrained families. Generally the two polar types of families (i.e., those in which both spouses made comparable assessments and both were either quite strained or experienced very little strain) were distinguished from one another most consistently.

Women in Strained and Unstrained Families

Salient characteristics of wives' employment varied somewhat by patterns of family strain from those of their husbands in that substantially fewer of the work attributes of women distinguished among the types of families. Like their spouses, wives in strained households were considerably younger than those in calmer families. For example, women in strained families averaged 34 years of age compared to 46 years for those in the least-stressed family environments. Despite being younger, there was a slight tendency for women in the most-strained families to be in higher-level occupations. This may reflect the entry of younger women into demanding occupations. Occupational level was the only employment characteristic of women that differentiated between pat-

Table 3.4

Depressive Symptoms and Employment Characteristics of Husbands and Wives in One- and Two-Job Families (Multiple Regression Analyses)

Characteristics	Husbands in One-Job Families N = 130		Husbands in Two-Job Families N = 135		Wives in Two-Job Families N = 135	
	r	Beta	r	Beta	r	Beta
Occupation	-.26	-.18*	.14	.18*	-.16	-.09
Work-family strain	.35	.44***	.35	.30***	.07	.14
Income	-.30	-.13	.13	.23**	-.01	.07
Job satisfaction	-.32	-.18	-.26	-.23**	-.25	-.12
Hours per week	-.09	-.07	-.02	-.13	.11	.25**
Evaluation as earner	-.04	.04	-.17	-.10	-.14	-.20*
Comparative financial situation	-.19	-.12	-.11	-.17	-.32	-.32***
R^2	.36		.28		.23	

* $p < .10$
** $p < .05$
*** $p < .01$

terns of family strain. Thus, the work characteristics of husbands were more salient than those of their wives in distinguishing between types of family strain. In summary, strained families were those in which couples were younger, husbands worked more hours with less job satisfaction, despite their greater commitment to work relative to the family or nonoccupational activities, and wives were in somewhat more demanding occupations than their peers in less-stressful circumstances.

Employment Characteristics and Depressive Symptoms

Models including the work characteristics identified previously were used to answer questions about the relative importance of the factors for depressive symptoms of employed men and women. Separate models were estimated for men and women. Negative perceptions of their financial situation were especially distressing for employed women (Table 3.4). Financial deprivation relative to the benefits believed to accrue to others and the observation that they were less adequate in the provider role fostered depressive symptoms in women. The more time women spent at work not only created greater role strain but also independently contributed to depression. High role strain did not affect the depressive symptoms of employed women directly. Employed women may be socialized to expect considerable strain and interference between work and family, whereas men may not anticipate it and, when it does come, are more distressed by it.

In contrast to women, men were not directly depressed about spending more time in the labor force. Rather, spending more time at work created role strain that in turn was a highly significant factor in fostering depressive symptoms among men in both types of families. Men in two-job families tended to be more depressed if they were in higher-level occupations, although along with their occupational status they benefited from having higher job satisfaction ($r = .32$). Men in one-job families had fewer depressive symptoms if they were in higher-level occupations although occupational level had an opposite effect for men whose wives worked outside the home. It may be that demands of a higher-level occupation combined with their spouses' employment contributed to the negative effect for men in dual-earner families. Although only two variables were significant, the model explained the most variance in depression of men in one-job families (36 percent) compared to 23 and 28 percent for women and men in dual-earner families.

A similar analysis of depressive symptoms in homemakers was conducted. Their husbands' employment characteristics (occupational level, hours spent at work, income, job satisfaction, evaluation of his performance as a provider, and assessment of his comparative financial situation), number of children at home, wife's age, educational level, and role strain were included. Homemakers also indicated whether they would still choose homemaking as their primary role if they had the opportunity to make the choice again. Higher role strain ($r = .21$) and the observation that they would choose an occupation other than homemaking ($r = .15$) were determinants of depressive symptoms of wives in single-earner families ($R^2 = .15$). Neither subjective nor objective characteristics of their partners' employment directly affected the distress of these homemakers. Rather, homemakers felt burdened by role overload and the wish that they had made other choices. Homemakers and employed women, however, did not differ in the depressive symptoms they experienced ($t = .68$, NS).

DISCUSSION AND CONCLUSIONS

This chapter has focused on selected aspects of employment, both objective and subjective, to determine their implications for work-family strain and depressive symptoms among the employed in one- and two-job families. What was learned about the similarities and differences in the strain and distress experienced by the employed in the variant family patterns?

First, men with employed wives were not disadvantaged with respect to work-family strain or psychological distress although, confirming other literature, women in the two-job family were more strained and described more depressive symptoms than men regardless of family pattern. Anderson and Leslie (1989) also found that women reported more family life stress than was observed by men. The greater depression of women, however, was not attributable to their circumstances in a two-job family, because wives who were not employed were equally depressed (Keith & Schafer, 1980).

Overload has been a central dimension of the concept of role strain, and it was a significant source of work-family strain shared by these employed persons independent of gender or family structure. Spending more time at work was especially critical in fostering perceptions of interference between employment and family among men in two-job families although men whose wives were full-time homemakers also were strained when they devoted more time to work. Employed women were more strained if they spent a greater amount of time in the labor force but to a lesser extent than were men.

The finding that men in single-earner families were more disadvantaged by engaging in nontraditional gender-role behavior in the household deserves comment. It may be that expectations by full-time homemakers that their husbands should be involved in domestic tasks seem inequitable because the wives are not participants in paid work. Requests for such help may seem unwarranted, and consequently participation by husbands may represent the most nontraditional involvement and may be costly to them.

Beyond time spent at work, the factors that distressed these men differed by type of family pattern. Men with employed spouses were not distressed by their wives' role strain. Rather, employed women and men in one-job families were more responsive to the experiences of their partners and were demoralized by strain experienced by them. For the most part, subjective assessments of how they were earning income were more salient to well-being of those in two-job families. In some instances, of course, concern over finances may have been one of the primary factors leading initially to their dual employment.

Although it was possible to identify families in which both husbands and wives experienced higher strain, usually the employment characteristics of spouses were not highly correlated, suggesting that a coping mechanism may have been for them to have dissimilar orientations and patterns of work behavior. For example, those highly committed to work and who spent a large part of their lives involved in it may have managed a two-job life-style by being married to someone with markedly different interests, at least to those for whom their job was not quite so all-consuming. This suggests that the career of one spouse, and not always that of the wife, may be designated by the couple as secondary to that of the other. Such decisions, whether intentional or derived in a less-systematic way, likely will have implications for perceptions of fairness or equity in the intimate relationship. The outcomes of equity or inequity for the well-being of men and women over the family life stages are observed in chapter 4.

4

Equity in the Marriage Relationship

In chapter 3 we investigated general evaluations of work, finances, and family patterns and their effects on well-being of employed spouses. In this chapter we turn to the marital relationship; we query husbands and wives about fairness and equity in their dealings with their partners and observe their consequences. As a general theory of social interaction, equity theory has implications for the study of the marital relationship and well-being over the family life stages. Equity theory has been used successfully to study exploiter/victim relationships, helping relationships, business or work relationships, and intimate relationships (Walster, Walster & Berscheid, 1978). The basic premise of equity theory is that individuals evaluate their inputs (contributions) and/or outcomes (consequences) in a relationship to determine the fairness or equity of their circumstances. Inequity will be felt if the individual's outcomes are either higher or lower than those of his or her partner. To restore actual equity to a relationship, the individuals can increase or decrease their own or their partners' inputs or outcomes. Individuals can restore psychological equity by distorting their own reality so that greater or lesser inputs or outcomes are perceived for either themselves or their partners.

The importance of equity/inequity to the well-being of marriage partners is suggested by one of the major propositions of equity theory that has implications for an intimate relationship. "When individuals find themselves participating in inequitable relationships, they become distressed. The more inequitable the relationship, the more distress the individuals feel" (Walster, Walster & Berscheid, 1978:6). When individuals are in an inequitable relationship, they feel uneasy about the relationship. This occurs for both the overbenefited, who are getting more from the relationship than they think they deserve, and the underbenefited, who are getting less than they think they deserve. According to Homans (1974) and Walster & Berscheid (1978), the overbenefited will feel guilt because of their favored position and the underbenefited will feel anger and resentment because they are not getting what they think they deserve. Participants in an equitable relationship feel comfortable and do not experience the distress associated with an inequitable relationship. Support for the proposition that both overbenefited and underbenefited persons feel distress in an inequitable relationship is provided in studies on casual interactions (Austin & Walster, 1974), as well as in an investigation of intimate relationships (Sprecher, 1986). There is further theorizing and evidence that persons who are underbenefited experience greater distress than those who are overbenefited (Walster & Berscheid, 1978). Whereas both experience the distress of inequity, the overbenefited receive an advantage from the relationship, but the underbenefited receive no such comfort.

For some, intimate relationships are considered to be "special" relationships that cannot be subjected to the calculations of input, outcome, and gain. They argue that intimate relationships transcend the concerns for equity and exchange that would characterize business or more formal relationships. Rubin (1973), for example, believes that the principles of exchange are likely to apply only to the developmental stages of a relationship and would not apply to a firmly bonded relationship. Also, Clark & Mills (1979) suggest that there is a distinction between relationships based on the mutual exchange of benefits and those based on providing benefits determined by the need of others for a benefit.

However, contrary to concerns about intimate relationships as "special" and devoid of calculations of gain or loss, research has provided ample evidence that principles of equity do indeed operate in intimate close personal relationships and have significant effects on the quality of the relationship. Crohan and Veroff (1989) found that equity, happiness, competence, and control were major factors in defining what constitutes well-being among both black and white newlyweds. A number of studies have supported the application of the central proposition of equity theory that equity or inequity has an effect on satisfaction or distress in close personal or marital relationships (Cate, Lloyd, Henton & Larson, 1982; Davidson, 1984; Sprecher, 1986). In addition, some investigators have broadened the application of equity in intimate relationships to consider the effect of equity on relationship commitment (Walster, Walster & Traupmann, 1978; Utne, Hatfield, Traupmann & Greenberger, 1984; Sabatelli & Cecil-Pigo, 1985). Equity theory, therefore, has been found to be a viable perspective to explain both satisfaction and commitment in close personal relationships.

The equity framework also has informed the study of a second aspect of social relationships, that of mate selection (Berscheid, Walster & Walster, 1971; Murstein, 1972; White, 1980; Walster, Walster & Traupmann, 1978). The empirical question examined in these studies is whether a concern for equity is a factor in determining whom a person will date or marry. As used in this context, equity becomes a theoretical explanation for the matching hypothesis. In the study of social attraction, the matching hypothesis has enjoyed a degree of popularity and has generated a substantial body of research. As a theory of social attraction it asserts that men and women of similar attractiveness are drawn to one another as romantic partners (Kalick & Hamilton, 1986). The popularity of this perspective may, in part, be due to the possibility that individuals may not seek out the most-attractive partner in a romantic relationship but indeed may prefer someone who is less attractive if it constitutes a match (Walster, Berscheid & Walster, 1976).

When couples are mismatched in attractiveness, the less-attractive partner must "negotiate" with the more-attractive partner over resources to compensate for the dissimilarity in attractiveness. An example of this would be an exchange of the security and social status of the less-attractive partner to secure the attentions of the more-attractive partner. This negotiation over the inequity of physical attraction introduces strain and tension into the relationship (Murstein, 1976). Therefore equity theory would suggest that individuals will avoid the stress and tension of a mismatched relationship by selecting partners who match them in physical attractiveness.

Whereas equity has been found to be a factor in attraction in close relationships, it has also been observed that couples who felt they matched in attractiveness were more content and happier. Berscheid, Walster, and Bohrnstedt (1973) asked dating and married respondents to rate their partners as compared to themselves. Respondents who rated their partners on the same level of attractiveness as they rated themselves were more satisfied with their relationship than respondents who rated their partners either more desirable or less desirable.

In this analysis of equity and well-being over the family life cycle, the effect of equity both in the marriage relationship and in mate selection is investigated. To accomplish this, four separate analyses will be conducted: first, there will be a general assessment of equity in the marital relationship; second, equity in critical marital roles across the family life stages will be considered; third, the relationship between inequity in marital roles and psychological distress will be studied; and fourth, physical similarity as a basis for attraction will be examined.

A GENERAL ASSESSMENT OF EQUITY IN THE MARITAL RELATIONSHIP

The initial step in studying equity in the marital relationship was to assess the general evaluation of equity by marriage partners. Couples made a universal assessment (Hatfield, 1978) of the fairness of their marital relationship (see chapter 2). Those respondents who felt the relationship was not fair because they were being taken advantage of were defined as "underbenefited." Those who felt their relationship was unfair because they believed they got a better deal than their partner were defined as "overbenefited." The couples' perception of equity and inequity is presented in Table 4.1. A high percentage of all husbands and wives at the different stages of the life cycle perceived equity in the marital relationship. Perceived equity tended to increase slightly over the life cycle, suggesting the accommodation that couples make to one another during their relationship. There was also a slight tendency for the partners at most of the life cycle stages who did not perceive equity to feel that they were overbenefited in the relationship. These findings suggest that for the marriage partners studied there was a generally favorable assessment of fairness in the relationship. This assessment seemed to change only modestly over the life stages.

This universal assessment of equity in the marital relationship provided a general picture of the perception of fairness by husbands and wives. However, this very limited analysis can only superficially capture the dynamics of the marital relationship. An analysis restricted to a general or universal assessment of equity would tend to obscure feelings about the fairness of specific aspects of the marriage relationship. Therefore, in the second component of the analysis we examine married couples' perceptions of their own and their spouses' efforts in performing selected family roles.

ASSESSMENT OF EQUITY IN SPECIFIC MARITAL ROLES

In a marriage, there are expectations as to who should perform family roles and assessments of the quality of the performance. It is likely that married couples make determinations about the equity of their own and their partners' performance in these roles. For this investigation, roles that were integral to the functioning of the family unit were chosen as the subject for the examination of perceptions of equity. Frequently performed roles that are necessary to the daily maintenance of the family presumably will be salient to marital partners, thus making it possible to elicit perceptions of equity. Inclusion of a variety of roles provides an opportunity to assess equity in situations requiring different types of skills.

Table 4.1
Spousal Perception of Equity or Inequity in Their Marriage Relationship

	Husbands				Wives			
Perception	Stage 1 N = 85	Stage 2 N = 88	Stage 3 N = 81	Stage 4 N = 82	Stage 1 N = 85	Stage 2 N = 88	Stage 3 N = 81	Stage 4 N = 82
Inequity over- benefited	23%	18%	20%	15%	12%	19%	13%	6%
Equity	72%	76%	74%	84%	70%	72%	79%	85%
Inequity under- benefited	5%	6%	6%	1%	18%	9%	8%	9%

Whereas there is little previous research on the question of equity across the life stages, predictions were drawn from Davis's (1973) theorizing on intimate relationships that the calculation of input and outcome is diminished in long-term intimate relationships. Beyond a certain point, "the closest of friends (as well as most lovers and spouses) do not feel obligated to give or expect to receive a specific repayment for each service rendered; rather each feels the total amount of favors he gives and receives will average out over the course of the friendship" (Davis, 1973:132). Following this reasoning, it is likely that, over the course of the marital career, adjustments and accommodations are made resulting from the reduction in the amount of consideration being given to repayment for favors. This reduction accompanies the realization that favors given and received tend to average out over time. These adjustments made by marital partners may be reflected in their perception of equity in the marital relationship. Where the relationship is relatively new and involves the introduction of new role responsibilities, such as rearing children, there is likely to be an acute awareness of the inputs and outcomes for each partner and a greater awareness of the existence of inequity. As the relationship matures, it is less likely that there will be perceived inequity between partners. The findings of the general measure of equity support this point of view. It is assumed that partners' perceived equity in the performance of specific marital roles will increase and, conversely, that inequity will decrease over the family life cycle stages.

A second issue in the specific assessment of fairness involves the differences between the husbands' and wives' perceptions of equity in the performance of marital roles. Again, there is little direct evidence upon which a prediction can be based, although differences found between males and females in studies of social interaction are instructive. Sawyer (1966) noted that females are more generous than males in social interaction. Lane and Messe (1971) found that females were less self-interested than males. In a study of married couples, Murstein, Cerreto, and MacDonald (1977) also observed that females had a lower exchange orientation to the marital relationship than males. These earlier studies suggest definite differences between males and females in their orientation to exchange relationships. Females tend to be more generous, less self-interested, and less exchange-oriented in social relationships. Based on these findings it is predicted that wives have a higher threshold for perceiving inequity than husbands; they will be more likely than their husbands to perceive equity and less likely to believe that inequity was unfavorable to them.

Equity in the performance of the family roles of cooking, housekeeping, provider, companion, and parent was determined using the equity measure reported in chapter 2. Couples' responses are shown in

Table 4.2. The expectation that equity will increase over the life cycle was generally confirmed. There was a constant increase in perceived equity in the roles of cooking, homemaking, and provider by both husbands and wives across the life-cycle stages. There was also an increase in perceived equity in the parent role between the two life-cycle stages in which there were children in the home. The greatest increase in perceived equity in the roles of cooking, homemaking, and provider occurred between Stage 2 and Stage 3. This corresponds to the time when children leave home.

The one exception to the prediction of an increase in equity in the family roles was the companion role. For husbands, the change in equity over the family life cycle was curvilinear, with Stages 1 and 4 demonstrating lower levels of equity. This pattern was reversed for wives, with Stages 1 and 4 reflecting higher levels of equity and Stages 2 and 3 representing lower levels.

Among husbands, the difference in perceived equity and inequity from Stage 1 to Stage 2 was fairly small for the housekeeping and provider roles. There were greater differences for the cooking, companion, and parent roles, with each demonstrating a decline in feeling overbenefited and an increase in equity. Differences from Stage 2 to Stage 3 indicated a decline in the underbenefited with a corresponding increase in equity for the housekeeping role. Differences between Stages 3 and 4 were small for all but the companion role, in which there was a decline in perceived equity.

Over the life stages the number of husbands who perceived inequity that underbenefited them in each of the roles was relatively small and constant. Furthermore, a higher proportion of husbands than wives perceived inequity that overbenefited them. With the exception of the role of the companion, husbands' perceptions of favorable inequity decreased over the family life cycle.

Wives' perceived equity or inequity across the family life course presented a different pattern than that of the husbands. A larger number of wives felt underbenefited than overbenefited in cooking and housekeeping activities at the first stage of the family life cycle. Between Stage 1 and Stage 2, wives experienced an increase in being overbenefited in the cooking, housekeeping, and companion roles and a decline in being overbenefited in the provider role. From Stage 2 to Stage 3, there was a decline in feeling overbenefited and an increase in equity for the cooking, housekeeping, provider, and companion roles. Differences between Stage 3 and Stage 4 were greater for wives than for husbands. The greatest differences between the last two stages in the life cycle for wives were an increase in underbenefit and a corresponding decrease in overbenefit for the cooking and housekeeping roles.

A general conclusion that can be drawn was that a very high pro-

Table 4.2
Perceived Equity of Husbands' and Wives' Performance Efforts, in Selected Family Roles across the Family Life Stages

Family Roles	Stage 1		Stage 2		Stage 3		Stage 4	
	Husbands N = 85	Wives	Husbands N = 88	Wives	Husbands N = 81	Wives	Husbands N = 82	Wives
Cooking								
Inequity-Overbenefited	43%	12%	28%	30%	25%	17%	20%	6%
Equity	52%	59%	63%	61%	71%	74%	78%	78%
Inequity-Underbenefited	5%	29%	9%	9%	4%	9%	2%	16%
Housekeeping								
Inequity-Overbenefited	45%	20%	47%	28%	36%	18%	34%	5%
Equity	48%	51%	47%	57%	61%	73%	64%	78%
Inequity-Underbenefited	7%	29%	6%	15%	3%	9%	2%	17%
Provider								
Inequity-Overbenefited	24%	37%	16%	24%	16%	8%	11%	10%
Equity	75%	61%	78%	69%	85%	88%	86%	86%
Inequity-Underbenefited	1%	2%	6%	7%		4%	3%	3%
Companion								
Inequity-Overbenefited	32%	21%	24%	31%	27%	24%	36%	13%
Equity	63%	73%	73%	63%	72%	71%	62%	84%
Inequity-Underbenefited	5%	6%	3%	6%	1%	5%	2%	3%
Parent								
Inequity-Overbenefited	39%	11%	32%	10%	NA	NA	NA	NA
Equity	57%	67%	67%	73%				
Inequity-Underbenefited	4%	22%	1%	17%				

portion of husbands and wives felt that there was equity in the performance of family roles and that this equity increased over the life stages (Table 4.2). Furthermore, those respondents who felt inequity were more likely to feel that it was in their favor, rather than benefiting their spouse. The finding that equity increases over the family life cycle from both a universal and a role-specific assessment is explained in part by Davis (1973) who, as noted before, maintains that, in long-term intimate relationships, less emphasis is placed on give-and-take and the calculation of services and favors. The increase of equity and the corresponding reduction of inequity that is either favorable or unfavorable would reflect the mutual adjustments and accommodations made in the marital relationship.

There are, however, other explanations that derive from the husband-wife relationship that need to be considered in order to explain the increases in perceived equity over time. The maturing marriage relationship requires a shift from the partners thinking in terms of "you" and "me" to a sense of "we-ness." This sense of "we-ness" is the result, in part, of the intertwining of the outcomes of intimates. As Blau (1964:77) noted, "the repeated experience of being rewarded by the increased attachment of a loved one after having done a variety of things to please him may have the effect that giving pleasure to loved ones becomes intrinsically gratifying." Through identification and empathy, marriage partners come to define themselves as a unit. They do not see themselves solely as interacting individuals but also as a partnership interacting with other partnerships (Walster, Walster & Berscheid, 1978). This sense of "we-ness" may tend to shift the concern for equity away from the husband-wife relationship between spouses to the relationship as a unit or partnership. As Walster, Walster, and Berscheid (1978:153) speculate, "this characteristic may have a dramatic impact on intimates' perception of what is and what is not equitable." The impact of acting as a partnership may be a factor in the increase found in the perception of equity in role performance over the family life cycle.

Whereas the data clearly indicated that perceived equity increased over the family life cycle, it was also evident that most partners of both sexes found their marriage imbalanced in their favor when it was not equitable. This suggests that equity may be related to marital adjustment. The more marriage partners perceive equity or the favorable position of being overrewarded in their relationship, the greater their marital satisfaction and adjustment may be. Fairness in a marriage relationship may be a component of marital adjustment that has not been adequately taken into account in past investigations.

A second issue we considered was the difference between the husbands and wives in their perception of equity and inequity (Table 4.3). It is evident that there are differences between spouses in their percep-

Table 4.3

Differences in Perceived Equity/Inequity in Performance of Family Roles by Sex and Family Life Stage (Chi-square)

Family Roles	Stage 1 N = 85	Stage 2 N = 88	Stage 3 N = 81	Stage 4 N = 82
Cooking	30.280***	.027	3.163	18.830***
Housekeeping	19.766***	7.347*	8.954*	28.047***
Provider	3.752	1.991	5.066	2.001
Companion	2.609	1.783	6.908	10.522***
Parent	26.117***	22.210***	N/A	N/A

*p. < .05
**p. < .01
***p. < .001

tions of equity and inequity. The differences, however, were opposite to those that had been predicted. The general pattern was one in which a higher proportion of wives than husbands perceived they were underbenefited and, conversely, a higher proportion of husbands than wives perceived they were overbenefited. Using a chi-square analysis in nine of the eighteen relationships between sex and equity, there was a significant difference between husbands and wives and their perception of equity or inequity. The significant chi-squares reflected agreement between spouses that husbands were overbenefited and that wives were underbenefited. In the nine relationships that were not significant, there was a trend toward perceptions of unfavorable inequity by wives. These nonsignificant chi-square values reflected a lack of agreement in the perception of the spouses as to who was being overbenefited and underbenefited.

For the younger families (Stage 1), there was a very clear difference between spouses' perceptions of equity and inequity in performance of cooking, housekeeping, and parenting. In the two roles that are traditionally performed by women, cooking and housekeeping, a high percentage of the husbands felt that inequity existed but that it was in their favor. To restore equity, they indicated that either they would have to increase their efforts or their wives would have to decrease theirs. This was also true of the shared roles of parent and companion. The proportion of wives feeling underbenefited in the roles of cooking, housekeeping, and parenting was greater than the proportion of those who felt that the inequity was in their favor. This may reflect the changing expectation in young families that husbands share more of these responsibilities with their wives. It may also be indicative of the stress and lower marital satisfaction that results from the introduction of a child into the family. Because husbands are less involved in the earlier years of child care, there are increased demands on wives in a number of family and household roles during this stage. Increases in role demands for the wife are likely to be recognized by both spouses.

At Stage 2 and Stage 3, the differences between husbands' and wives' perceptions of equity diminished, although there were still differences for the role of housekeeper, in both stages, and for parent roles among younger couples. But even here the differences in the proportions were not as great as for Stage 1 couples.

For older respondents (Stage 4), the differences between husbands' and wives' perceptions of equity tended to increase for cooking, housekeeping, and companion roles. This resulted in a curvilinear pattern over the life stages in which the proportion of wives perceiving inequity that overbenefited them decreased and those perceiving inequity that underbenefited them increased for cooking and housekeeping roles at Stage 4. Also, the proportion of husbands perceiving equity for the companionship role decreased at Stage 4.

This finding suggests that while women have been found to be more generous and less self-interested and to have a lower exchange orientation than males, it does not necessarily mean that they are more likely to perceive equity in the marital relationship. The dynamics of the family, especially having a child for young couples and retirement for older couples, introduce elements into the marital relationship that affect the equity of role performance. These structural factors probably transcend psychological differences between the sexes in fostering perceptions of equity. Furthermore, with the increase in work outside the home and the assumed trend toward more liberal sex-role orientations, women's expectations for equity in the home may have increased. But changes in relationships between men and women have occurred unevenly in various sectors of life (Fogarty, Rapoport & Rapoport, 1971). Equity in male-female relationships has been much more pronounced in the occupational sphere, for example, than in the family, with women still taking major responsibility for household tasks (Schafer & Schafer, 1989). This may in part explain why young women, who are more likely to be faced with both child-rearing and employment demands, especially report perceptions of being underbenefited.

At the other end of the life cycle, in the retirement family, wives also feel underbenefited. This may be explained partially by the retirement of the husband, placing him back into the family, or perhaps the retirement of both spouses and the necessity to renegotiate allocations of responsibility.

In addition to the influences of specific structural conditions of the various family life stages, an alternative explanation for the differences between husbands and wives is provided by the studies on coalition formation by Vinacke and his associates. In this research, females allocated rewards differently than males (Bond & Vinacke, 1961; Vinacke & Gullickson, 1964). Females tended to be accommodating in their allocation of rewards. Their major concern was the maintenance of harmonious personal relationships in which the welfare of all members was protected. Males, on the other hand, tended to adopt a more exploitive strategy in their interaction with others. Their main concern was the protection of their own interests. These different strategies in the approach to exchange and the allocation of rewards may indeed be a factor in the evaluation of equity in the performance of family roles. If males are exploitive, then husbands may recognize the exploitive nature of the allocation of rewards in the marital relationship. Therefore, they would be more likely than women to feel that they are overbenefited in the relationship and need to increase their efforts to restore equity. The wives may attempt to maintain a harmonious relationship, but may also recognize the differences between them and their spouses in allocating rewards. Therefore, the wives may be more likely than husbands to feel that they are underbenefited in the relationship and that they need to decrease efforts or their spouses need to increase their efforts in order to make the relationship fair.

INEQUITY AND PSYCHOLOGICAL DISTRESS

Although there was a clear tendency for the couples in this study to perceive equity rather than inequity in the performance of roles, a further question needs to be considered: "Did those who experienced inequity in marital roles also experience psychological distress in their relationships?" As has been noted, a major prediction of equity theory is that when individuals participate in an inequitable relationship they experience distress, and the more inequitable the relationship the greater the distress. The existence of inequity in a marital relationship has implications for the well-being of the partners in that relationship.

Marriage is a relatively long-term relationship in which considerable investments are made and which would be somewhat costly to terminate. Marriage partners are indeed significant others, having real biographical importance in each others' lives. It is likely that in such a relationship the anger from being underbenefited and the guilt from being overbenefited would have implications not just for unhappiness with the relationship but also for the general psychological well-being of the participants. Inequity in the performance of roles that are part of this relationship may produce strains that continue over time and foster psychological distress. Indeed, as noted by Hinchcliffe, Hooper, and

Roberts (1978), depressive behavior in the family becomes the end product of a series of interactional problems and misunderstandings. Will
inequity in a long-term, intimate relationship have an impact so great
as to affect psychological well-being? To determine this, the relationship
between inequity and depression for each of the marital roles was
examined.

The relationships between equity and depressive symptoms for the
five different family roles are presented in Table 4.4. The average depression scores give consistent evidence that marriage partners who felt
either overbenefited or underbenefited in the performance of marital
roles experienced greater psychological distress than marriage partners
who perceived equity. Husbands and wives who felt that there was
equity in the performance of each of the roles showed fewer depressive
symptoms than respondents who felt either overbenefited or
underbenefited.

F-tests were conducted to examine both linear trends and quadratic
effects above linear trends for equity and inequity. This enables us to
determine whether the relationship between depression and equity is
linear or curvilinear, with high depression scores for overbenefited and
underbenefited and lower depression scores for those experiencing equity. The only significant linear trends were for husbands' evaluation
of equity in the cooking and parent roles. There were significant quadratic effects above linear trends for each of the husbands' roles and for
each of the wives' roles except their evaluations of the provider and
companion roles. Thus, the pattern of quadratic relationships in which
the overbenefited and underbenefited reported higher depression scores
was relatively consistent across family roles for both partners.

The data were analyzed further to determine whether the quadratic
effects were a function of sex or the number of years of marriage. The
only significant effect for length of marriage was for husbands' perceptions of the equity in the housekeeping role and wives' perceptions of
equity in the cooking role. In general, with the two noted exceptions,
it did not seem that the quadratic effects were affected by the length of
marriage. Examining the effects of sex, the data provided no evidence
that quadratic effects were significantly different for husbands and
wives.

It was found that wives experienced greater depression, in both equitable and inequitable relationships, than did husbands for each of the
five roles. This is consistent with earlier research, which suggests that
women generally report greater psychological distress than men. Length
of marriage, however, did not have a significant effect on the depression
scores for any of the five roles.

It was also found that marriage partners who felt overbenefited in the
performance of roles were less distressed than those who felt under-

Table 4.4

Relationship between Equity and Inequity in the Performance of Family Roles and Depressive Symptoms

Family Roles	Mean Depression Scores (X) (N in parentheses)		F Values						
	Husband	Wife	Linear Trend for Equity		Quadratic Trend above Equity Linear		Effect of Years Married on Quadratic Trend		Effect of Sex on Quadratic Trend
			Husband	Wife	Husband	Wife	Husband	Wife	
Cooking									
Underbenefited	2.33 (17)a	2.39 (53)	4.46 (1/330)c	.08	14.24*** (1/330)c	9.79***	1.03 (6/321)c	5.28***	.39 (2/660)c
Equity	1.99 (219)	2.24 (226)							
Overbenefited	2.10 (97)	2.41 (54)							
Housekeeping									
Underbenefited	2.24 (16)b	2.44 (59)	1.53 (1/330)c	.86	10.46*** (1/330)c	11.05***	2.31* (6/321)c	1.70	.37 (2/660)c
Equity	1.97 (181)	2.24 (214)							
Overbenefited	2.10 (136)	2.36 (60)							
Provider									
Underbenefited	2.25 (8)b	2.29 (15)	.01 (1/325)c	.16	8.19** (1/325)c	.50	.45 (6/316)c	.97	1.31 (2/650)c
Equity	1.99 (266)	2.28 (251)							
Overbenefited	2.21 (54)	2.35 (62)							
Companion									
Underbenefited	2.37 (10)	2.57 (16)	3.74 (1/330)c	2.89	11.40*** (1/330)c	8.85***	.84 (6/321)c	1.40	.13 (2/660)c
Equity	1.99 (225)	2.25 (242)							
Overbenefited	2.11 (98)	2.36 (75)							
Parent									
Underbenefited	2.50 (4)b	2.34 (34)	4.17* (1/170)c	.01	8.32*** (1/170)c	1.87	1.50 (2/167)c	1.43	2.45 (2/340)c
Equity	1.98 (108)	2.25 (121)							
Overbenefited	2.08 (61)	2.35 (18)							

a The higher the number, the more depressed a respondent feels.
b The difference in numbers are due to nonresponses to this question.
  The lower numbers for the parent role occur because of the number of households included in the sample in which there were no children in the home.
c Degrees of freedom for husbands and wives.
*p <.05
**p <.01
***p <.001.

benefited. The differences in depression scores were not large and the Scheffe multiple-range test indicated that the differences between the overbenefited and underbenefited were not significant at the .05 level of probability.

Whereas the largest proportion of partners perceived equity in the performance of family roles, those husbands and wives who perceived that they were either overbenefited or underbenefited had higher depressive symptom scores than those who perceived equity. These results are consistent with earlier studies, which indicate that equitable relationships are comfortable while inequitable relationships are distressing. However, the findings suggested that inequity was so salient a dimension in a long-term intimate relationship that its presence was associated with depressive symptoms. Therefore, in addition to the correspondence between the present study and earlier investigations of equity and inequity and distress, we need to consider further explanations for the findings that center on psychological distress.

In developing a theoretical perspective on depression, Beck (1967, 1974) located the root of depression as a negative cognitive set. The depressed person has a negative view of self, of the world, and of the future. These negative cognitions are primary and influence the state of depression. It is, therefore, the individual's perception and appraisal of external events and circumstances that produce depression.

Beck's cognitive theory of depression has implications for the current investigation. Because of the importance and relative permanence of marriage, inequity in the relationship will have a significant impact on the psychological well-being of the participants. Partners who are underbenefited may feel frustration and disappointment in the marital relationship. They are experiencing inequity in the day-to-day activities of a relationship that is socially defined as important and one they cannot easily leave. Also, because the underbenefited are victims, they may experience a diminished sense of self-worth. Therefore, being underbenefited in a long-term, intimate relationship may cause the marriage partners to make negative judgments about their situation, their future, the relationship, and themselves. These negative evaluations may result in increased depression.

On the other hand, respondents who are overbenefited are expected to experience self-concept distress (Walster & Berscheid, 1978). When one spouse is overbenefited at the expense of the other, this violates ethical principles that the relationship should be fair and conflicts with self-expectations. The resulting self-concept distress is a negative cognitive stage that may induce depressive symptoms.

This analysis again demonstrates the importance of equity as a predictor of psychological well-being in intimate relationships. Whereas equity is clearly a factor to be considered in the study of well-being, recent research in family stability and dissolution has pointed to another exchange variable that has implications for satisfaction in intimate relationships. There is accumulating evidence that the presence or absence of a favorable alternative to a particular relationship is a more important determinant of the stability or dissolution of a relationship than is perceived equity (Michaels, Acock & Edwards, 1986; Sprecher, 1986; Felmlee, Sprecher & Bassin, 1990).

EQUITY AND MATCHING

Although equity has been found to be an important factor in the couple relationships studied and in the psychological well-being of the couples, there are also other applications of equity theory in a close relationship. Equity considerations may also figure in the initial stages of what later become long-term intimate relationships. The matching hypothesis, which proposes that individuals of roughly similar levels of attractiveness are drawn together as romantic partners, assumes an equity explanation. Individuals avoid the inequity and related stress of a mismatched relationship by selecting a partner similar to them in physical attractiveness. Following the predictions of the matching hypothesis, we attempt to determine whether physical matching was an element in the partner selection of the couples. Like earlier research, this is a correlational study in which physical similarities of couples in existing relationships were observed. Unlike earlier studies, however, we will not focus on a traditional conception of physical attractiveness.

Our objective is to investigate one aspect of the matching hypothesis not often examined in isolation: Are men and women of the same weight classification attracted as romantic partners? Although matching in size and weight has been suggested as theoretically important for mate selection and for partners remaining together (Hatfield & Sprecher, 1986), there has been relatively little empirical investigation of romantic partners who are similar in weight classification. Whereas weight is not unrelated to the question of physical attractiveness and has sometimes been incorporated in the measure of attractiveness (White, 1980), this analysis proposes to study the matching of couples on the basis of weight alone. The appropriateness of this focus is supported by research on the attractiveness stereotype, in which it has been found that in the American culture weight is a factor in the assessment of physical attractiveness.

A second issue is whether matching by weight occurs over the family life stages. Previous research has demonstrated that couples who have been married longer show higher within-couple attractiveness correlations (Cavior & Boblett, 1972; White, 1980; Hill, Rubin & Peplau, 1976), while other research has postulated greater similarity in various characteristics of spouses across the life cycle (Chambers, Christiansen & Kunz, 1983). Whereas physical attractiveness and height are relatively stable factors, changes in weight can be controlled by the individual. Because weight can change, is there a tendency for matching to be sustained over the life cycle, or is there a tendency for partners to become mismatched? The first question assumes common life-styles and food behaviors that would contribute to matching by weight and is further articulated by Aron's (1988) suggestion for intracouple attractiveness correlations that "people may become more similar as a result of spending time together." The second question recognizes the reality of factors that can contribute to weight changes, such as childbirth, illness, gender, and individual weight preference.

The weight status used to determine matching of the subjects was the difference between the ideal weight and the actual weight. The ideal weight was based on four standard measures—weight, height, frame size, and sex. Respondents gave self reports of weight and height. Frame size was determined by measuring the diameter of the right wrist. To determine ideal weight for each subject, the 1983 Metropolitan Life Height-Weight tables were used. The tables provide weight ranges by height, sex, and frame size. Using the individual deviation from the midpoint of that range, respondents' weight status was calculated by subtracting their ideal weight from their reported weight. This calculation determined the number of spouses who were overweight or underweight or at the ideal weight. The comparisons of actual weight to ideal weight for subjects were used to determine intracouple correlations for subjects in the four life-stage samples.

Using the weight of spouses to examine the matching hypothesis, it was predicted that married couples would match on weight status. Inspection of Pearson's correlation coefficients revealed that young families at the first life-cycle stage conformed statistically to the prediction of the matching hypothesis. There was a modest tendency for younger couples in this study to have chosen romantic partners who were similar in weight classification ($r = .34, p < .001$). This matching, however, was not sustained during the next two life-cycle stages. There were not significant intracouple weight correlations for couples with older children in the home ($r = .04$) or for empty-nest couples ($r = .08$). For the elderly couples at the last life-cycle stage, there was again modest evidence of matching by weight ($r = .26, p < .01$).

A partial correlation analysis was used to determine the effect of socioeconomic status, childbirth, and concern for weight control on the intracouple correlations. First-order partial correlations controlling for family income, wives' and husbands' education, the number of children the wife had borne, and the wives' concern for weight control had no appreciable effect on the relationship between husbands' and wives' weight status. When all five mediating variables were controlled at once in a fifth-order partial correlation, they again had little effect on the intracouple correlations. Therefore, correlations between the weight of spouses were independent of socioeconomic status, bearing children, or concerns about weight control.

Because the significant correlations explained a small portion of the variance, the findings provided only limited support for the prediction derived from the matching hypothesis that there is similarity within married couples in weight classification. The findings for the younger couples in the sample were consistent with earlier studies which demonstrated significant intracouple attractiveness correlations (White, 1980; McKillip & Riedle, 1983). Explanations for matching by weight for the younger subjects can be drawn from equity theory. By selecting partners similar to them in weight, they avoid negotiations over inequity and the strains and tension associated with such negotiations. They have chosen partners of approximately their own social worth.

The second question was to determine whether matching by weight was sustained at different life-cycle stages. The cross-sectional analysis provided tentative evidence of a curvilinear relationship with matching by weight for the young and the elderly couples, but not for the middle-aged couples. There was evidence that couples did not grow more similar in appearance, at least as assessed by weight status, the longer they had been married. This finding is consistent with the research of Chambers et al. (1983) and Griffith and Kunz (1973), who found no support for the hypothesis that married couples tend to become physically more alike over time.

The matching effects found for younger couples may reflect more recent selection conditions that occurred at the initial stages of interaction. However, attraction effects that may have produced matching in weight for Stage 2 and Stage 3 couples early in their relationship may have been negated by changes in the weight status of one or the other partner over time. The significance of the intracouple weight correlations for the elderly couples suggests the possibility that a return to common life-styles may effect similar weight status. With retirement both partners are placed in the home, sharing meals and other activities. There is evidence that some gender-role characteristics of men and women may cross over or even merge in later life (Gutmann, 1975). Food habits and health consciousness as well may become more similar and be reflected in a tendency for weight to be similar. The shared experiences in retired families, which are less likely to characterize middle-aged couples, may result in the modest degree of weight matching found for the elderly subjects.

Support for this analysis of the findings is provided by the partial correlations, which demonstrated that matching by weight is generally independent of the mediating variables examined. Therefore, the matching by weight may reflect initial attraction (younger couples) or the effects of a shared life-style (retired couples) rather than the influence of social status, education, childbirth, or personal concern for weight control.

CONCLUSION

The findings presented in this chapter provide clear evidence for the importance of equity and inequity to the marital relationship and the psychological well-being of the marriage partners. There was a tendency for marriage partners to perceive equity rather than inequity in the performance of roles. Furthermore, perceived equity increased over the family life-cycle stages. The differences found between husbands and wives in perceived equity or inequity reflected changes in the family due to life-cycle adjustments and the impact of changing views and expectations for the performance of marital roles by husbands and wives. The findings also supported the notion that there is a reduced concern for repayment of favors in a marriage as the relationship matures. It was demonstrated that inequity in the performance of specific tasks in a marriage relationship is an important factor, with effects great enough to be associated with depression. We offer that notions of equity may figure in the selection of physical attributes, especially early in relationships, and we suggest equity as a proposed factor to account for mate selection based on weight status.

In this chapter we have considered the differential responses of husbands and wives to one aspect of the marital relationship—perceived equity or inequity in their contributions. In chapter 5, we begin with a more general discussion of gender roles across the life stages, with special attention to gender roles in the older family. Gender-role attitudes, expectations for gender roles, and actual behavior in the families across the life stages are investigated.

5

Gender Roles in the Family: Is the Older Family Different?

In this chapter we investigate gender roles and how they may differ over the life course, with particular focus on the older family. Our knowledge of gender roles across the life course is based on answers to a variety of questions that social scientists have asked persons about their lives. The information that we have includes age-appropriate expectations for gender-role behavior that individuals have for themselves and hold for others, expectations that they believe others have of them, reports of actual gender-role behavior in their daily routines, and assessments of their own masculine and feminine characteristics. Although some of the findings are contradictory, we now have information on these issues from persons at various places in the life course.

Several questions guide our investigation in this chapter: What does the social science literature say about gender roles in the family late in the twentieth century? Are there differences across the life course? Within families what do spouses expect of one another? In which work-family tasks are spouses actually involved over the life stages? To what extent are expectations and behavior gender-linked? Lastly, what are the outcomes of holding certain expectations about gender roles in the family and of acting on them?

In this chapter, these questions are addressed primarily in two ways. We (1) review selected social science research and writing on gender differentiation over the life course and (2) provide additional information from our studies of 336 couples in various life stages. For the most part we use the term *gender roles* rather than *sex roles*. Sex refers to physically defined categories, whereas the study of gender involves investigation of the meanings of maleness or femaleness in the social context (Kramer, 1991). Gender roles, then, are used to convey the sociocultural components of roles that are typically associated with males or females (Chafetz, 1978).

DEPICTION OF GENDER ROLES OVER THE LIFE COURSE IN SOCIAL SCIENCE LITERATURE

Much of the research and writing on gender differentiation throughout life, including that in older families, has reflected two general approaches. One body of research has been derived primarily from psychology and frequently includes self-assessments of gender-role characteristics. In efforts to describe aspects of gender roles across the life span, this research has included individuals from a variety of age groups ranging from adolescence through middle age (Sinnott, 1986).

To learn how persons describe themselves with regard to masculinity or femininity, this line of research often employs the Bem Sex Role Inventory (BSRI). Although we use the term gender role, sex role is widely used in psychology and sociology; when necessary for clarity or the context of a particular scholar's research, this usage will be retained (e.g., the Bem Sex Role Inventory).

Sometimes the same measures have been used to assess concepts with different labels. The same ratings of masculinity and femininity have been variously described as sex-role self-concept (Puglisi, 1983), sex-role identity (Puglisi, 1983), sex-role characteristics, and sex-role orientation (Windle, 1986). Regardless of their labels, data derived from this type of research are often based on choices of descriptive adjectives believed to represent masculine or feminine attributes. Examples of masculine characteristics include "assertive," "independent," and "forceful," whereas feminine items are represented by "compassionate," "affectionate," and "sensitive to needs of others." Presumably, it is assumed that persons are likely to behave in a manner congruent with their self-descriptions. Frequently this approach has been extended to identify those characteristics (e.g., masculine, feminine, androgynous) most often linked to indicators of well-being.

The second genre of research has focused on gender roles in the family and usually has been conducted by scholars in family studies and family sociology. Investigation of roles in the household has taken two general tacks. Some inquiries assess expectations that people have for their spouses in the household, frequently estimating the degree to which they believe that they should have responsibility for designated activities. In research that concentrates on the assignment of household tasks among couples, spouses are often asked to report who most usually (i.e., husband or wife) performs certain activities. The intent of some of this research is to estimate the extent to which household work is shared by spouses and how sharing may vary by the nature of the tasks considered. Just as there has been examination of the extent to which gender-role identity may be associated with well-being, there has been consideration of how shifts in the division of labor may impact the adjustment and well-being of spouses (Benin & Agostinelli, 1988; Brubaker, 1990; Hardesty & Bokemeier, 1989).

In the sections that follow, literature from these two dominant approaches—psychology and family studies—is reviewed. Current thinking on the nature of gender-role orientations across the life course from the psychological perspective is considered. This is followed by investigation of the nature of gender-role differentiation in the household, including that of older families. Throughout, attention is directed to evidence of gender-role differentiation, both in concepts of the self as masculine, feminine, or androgynous and in the tasks assumed in the household over the life span. Following the review, information on gender-role expectations and behavior of spouses in four age groups are analyzed and discussed.

Psychological Dimensions of Gender-Role Orientation

Prior to the 1970s, masculinity and femininity were conceptualized as opposite points on a single bipolar continuum; greater masculinity implied lesser femininity and vice versa (Betz & Fitzgerald, 1987). This view extended the notion of opposite biological sexes to include opposite personality traits as well. Failure to conform to gender roles appropriate to one's biological sex was indicative of psychopathology. Yet, as research revealed that the feminine role was seen as both less socially desirable and less healthy, use of the bipolar model seemed to have highly negative consequences for women (Betz & Fitzgerald, 1987).

In early research, masculinity and femininity were conceptualized as separate dimensions, independent of one another. In this view, individuals could have high levels of both masculinity and femininity, a high level of one and a low level of the other, or low levels of both.

Since Bem's (1974) introduction of the BSRI to measure sex-role orientation, numerous studies have considered various psychological characteristics of "masculine," "feminine," "androgynous," and "undifferentiated" sex-typed individuals. Bem postulated that androgynous individuals (i.e., those with a balance of masculine and feminine characteristics), by virtue of their ability to draw on a variety of gender-role behaviors, would have maximal behavioral flexibility, adaptability, and greater psychological well-being.

In an extensive review of this research Cook (1985) found that androgyny was related to flexibility in gender-role behavior (Orlofsky & Windle, 1978), assertion skills (Campbell, Steffen & Langmeyer, 1981) and high self-esteem (Spence, Helmreich & Stapp, 1975). Gender-typed orientations had different outcomes including low anxiety for masculine respondents (Erdwins, Small & Gross, 1980) whereas femininity resulted in low self-esteem for men (Jones, Chernovetz & Hansson, 1978) and low activity, extraversion, and emotional stability for women (Thomas & Reznikoff, 1984).

It must be noted, however, that a large proportion of the research on various aspects of gender-role orientation has tended to sample young adults who are often college undergraduates. At the other end of the life cycle, two types of research have been dominant. One focus of research has been primarily on changes in or a reversal of gender roles in old age, and a second emphasis has centered on the relationship between gender-role orientation and a variety of indices of well-being.

One perspective posits not only a change in gender roles over time but a reversal of gender roles at older ages. Following this theme, it has been proposed that women, once freed from their active parental role, are apt to display more masculine traits; whereas men, experiencing changes in the provider and work role, no longer need to espouse masculine behavior and are therefore more likely to display feminine traits, suggesting the notion of a sex-role reversal in later life (Gutmann, 1980; Livson, 1983; McGee & Wells, 1982; Nash & Feldman, 1981). Similarly, other changes may occur that are linked to self-conceptions and family roles. In their study of pre- and post–empty-nest women, Cooper and Gutmann (1987) found that the women in the latter stage saw themselves as having more self-confidence, independence, assertiveness, problem-solving capabilities, and creativity. Responding to an open-ended measure of gender identity, post–empty-nest women viewed themselves as having more masculine traits than their counterparts still actively involved in child rearing. Other differences were found between the two groups when the Thematic Apperception Test (TAT) was used; post–empty-nest women were significantly different in the active or active-bimodal ego-mastery styles. In terms of the family life stages, however, parenting roles may be less important in influencing masculine/feminine behavior than the employment or educational status of the female partner.

Not all research confirms the concept of gender-role reversal in older men and women. Rather, there is some evidence that tends to support the adoption of androgynous characteristics in later life. For example, Sinnott (1984) asked aged respondents to rate themselves using the BSRI and to denote the expectations they thought others had for their gender-role behavior. It was found that men and women portrayed themselves in both masculine and feminine terms, thereby supporting the notion of increased androgyny. Respondents also pointed out that they believed others expected them to behave in an androgynous manner as well.

Still, although androgyny has been found in some older adult samples, other research presents evidence of different gender-typing, especially among older women. In a comparison of older adults, younger adults, and college students on Bem's Sex Role Inventory, Sinnott (1982) observed that older women had the highest femininity scores of all groups, including men and women of other ages. Similarly, Erdwins, Tyer, and Mellinger (1983) noticed that married women 60 to 75 years old who had at least one child were highest on feminine traits, when compared with younger and middle-aged women. These findings and those on androgyny suggest that a reversal does not occur for all older women.

Whereas the issue of gender-role changes in later life is still being weighed, other research has investigated the relationship between gender-role orientation and the psychological adjustment or well-being of the aged. Often such research has tended to consider various outlooks on life (e.g., depressive symptoms and life satisfaction) in relation to gender-role orientation. In keeping with Bem's original assumption that androgynous individuals would exhibit better psychological adjustment, Sinnott (1982) observed that older men and women who were androgynous had better mental health. In addition, Shichman and Cooper (1984) also found general life satisfaction was higher for androgynous persons in comparison to other gender types. In this research a sample of respondents aged 17 to 74 were studied. In an investigation of middle-aged males, Downey (1984) found androgyny to be associated with higher levels of self-rated health status.

Nevertheless, the research establishing androgyny as the ideal sex-type in later life lacks consensus. Frank, Towell, and Huyck (1985), for example, observed that masculine respondents in their sample of women aged 47 to 68 years reported higher measures on self-esteem. Other researchers studying persons of various ages have found masculinity associated with low levels of depression (Morgan, Affleck & Riggs, 1986; Whitley, 1984).

There does, however, seem to be greater consensus regarding outcomes of a feminine gender-type orientation in later life. Having a feminine gender-type orientation has been linked to a high degree of distress in women and low ratings of mental health for both men and women (Frank et al., 1985; Sinnott, 1982). Considering masculinity and femininity conjointly, women with high levels of masculinity, independent of their femininity, were less depressed (Whisman & Jacobson, 1989). Generally, then, masculinity has been correlated inversely with depression and femininity positively (Whisman & Jacobson, 1989; Whitley, 1984). Congruency in the degree to which spouses are gender-typed also may affect how they regard their marriages. Apparently younger couples who are both gender-typed enjoy less marital satisfaction than their androgynous peers (Zammichieli, Gilroy & Sherman, 1988).

A notable exception to these findings is Windle's (1986) observation about cognitive flexibility and life satisfaction in a sample of older men and women. Neither androgyny nor masculinity was associated with high levels of life satisfaction or flexibility. Finally, Sinnott (1984) found that depression was related to the conflict respondents felt between expected and actual roles. Therefore, the link between gender-role orientation and well-being may not be due to the direction of gender typing so much as to the degree of congruence between self-identity and the presumed expectations of others. In future research, these factors need to be evaluated in the same model.

Conclusions about the relationship between gender-role orientation and well-being must be regarded with caution. Although there is some variation in size, the majority of samples used in the study of gender-role orientation often have been opportunistic "convenience" samples (e.g., college classes, senior centers, friends and family of these respondents, and other volunteers), small, and limited geographically as well (e.g., participants in senior centers in rural areas). Observations based on probability samples are rare, and the lack of representativeness is a severe problem.

Although much of the research on perceptions of masculinity and femininity has been drawn from the Bem Sex Role Inventory, it should be noted that some researchers have questioned its usefulness with older adult samples (Hyde & Phillis, 1979; Windle, 1986; Windle & Sinnott, 1985). For example, the items were derived from samples of persons with higher levels of education than the current cohort of older adults, and the descriptive items used to differentiate gender-role type may be more applicable to earlier life stages. Next, we mention some of the available information about gender-role attitudes and behavior as they may vary by age. Whereas we used gender-role orientation to refer primarily to assessments of masculinity and femininity, gender-role attitudes denote respondents' views of the appropriate roles for men and women both within the household and in the workplace.

PERSPECTIVES ON GENDER ROLES IN YOUNGER AND OLDER FAMILIES

Various theoretical perspectives have been used to address the allocation of marital and household roles. Generally the theories have not taken into account the transitions that may accompany retirement and the potential changes that may occur in the older family. The question of interest then is, "Under what conditions do families behave in less traditional ways or in ways that may indicate change?" That is, what factors are linked with more-or-less modern gender-role behavior in the family, and how may it be explained?

The model most often used to explain the division of domestic work hinges on female participation in the labor force and takes into account available time of spouses, wives' employment, and gender-role attitudes (Hardesty & Bokemeier, 1989). A typical model (Kamo, 1988) posits that because wives in the labor force have less available time for housework, their spouses will increase the time they spend in the household. The gender-role ideology of husbands and wives includes their beliefs about the appropriateness of sharing paid employment and work in the household. In commonly used models it is assumed that, in families with more modern gender-role ideologies, husbands will have greater involvement in work in the household. Employment of both partners provides material resources. The thinking is that wives' employment, especially their resources, and the gender-role attitudes of both spouses jointly affect power in the marriage. It is theorized that as wives' power increases so will the amount of housework done by the husband. This then is a typical model, all or a part of which has been used frequently to explain the division of labor in the family (e.g., Kamo, 1988; Hardesty & Bokemeier, 1989).

In general, the fact that women are employed or the characteristics of their employment (e.g., hours per week spent in work) have little influence on the amount of housework undertaken by husbands (Berk, 1985; Crouter et al., 1987; Pleck, 1985). Relative to men in single-earner families, husbands of employed women spend more time in housework, but only because women engaged in paid work do less than full-time homemakers (Berardo et al., 1987). In response to the time they spend in paid work, women allocate less time to housework and childcare (Berardo et al., 1987).

Gender-Role Attitudes and Gender Roles in Younger and Older Families

Whereas the research reviewed earlier assessed some of the psychological attributes of gender-role orientations, other scholars have investigated attitudes toward gender roles, marital roles, and the division of labor in the family (Huber & Spitze, 1981; Ross, 1987). As noted, many of the conclusions regarding gender-role orientation have been based on samples of college students and young adults. Until recently there was less attention to actual gender roles, attitudes toward gender roles, and their consequences for older families. This lack may have been due to the underlying supposition that older couples continue with the same patterns of interaction they had when they were younger. Yet, research building on the framework of family development suggests that there is the least role differentiation among the newly married and the aged, with increased differentiation observed among families in the middle years with children (Mattessich & Hill, 1987). This, in part, parallels the supposition of Gutmann (1980) that freedom from parenting permits the manifestation of the "normal unisex of later life" exemplified in a tendency toward reversals in masculine and feminine traits. Even though actual role differentiation may be curvilinear, there likely will be transitions in attitudes toward gender roles that may or may not be reflected in behavior in the family.

Shifts in Gender-Role Attitudes. Several studies have observed shifts in gender-role attitudes toward more egalitarian expectations with regard to both female employment outside the household and the division of labor within the family. The greatest changes have been documented among women, younger persons, urban residents, and higher socio-economic status groups (Scanzoni & Arnett, 1987; Szinovacz, 1984). McBroom (1986), for example, investigated changing gender-role orientations in a sample of women aged 23 to 52 over a five-year period. It was found that the young-adult cohort (age 23 to 32) had the greatest change away from a traditional gender-role orientation, followed by the oldest cohort (age 42 to 52), and lastly the adult cohort (age 33 to 41). For these women such life events as marriage, divorce, separation, and employment diminished gender-role traditionalism. All cohorts, however, experienced some decrease in traditionalism. In a comparison of three generations of women and their attitudes toward women, Dambrot, Papp, and Whitmore (1984) found students were more liberal whereas their grandmothers were more conservative.

Gender Roles in the Older Family. Despite transitions toward less-traditional gender-role attitudes, the typical household division of labor consists of feminine tasks (e.g., cooking, laundry) and of masculine activities (e.g., lawn work, car maintenance, and home repairs), with the responsibility for such activities generally remaining gender-typed (Whicker & Kronenfeld, 1986). This continues to be the dominant pattern today (Nyquist, Slivken, Spence & Helmreich, 1985) just as it was twenty years earlier (Duncan & Duncan, 1978; Pleck, 1983; Szinovacz, 1989). Thus, for the most part, this gender-typed allocation of labor in the household has extended over time and across life-course cohorts into the later years, with wives of retirees and retired women continuing to perform most of the housework (Brubaker, 1990).

A frequently stated concern, but one not often addressed with anything beyond speculation, is whether behavior in older families is a departure from what occurred earlier in their life together. One longitudinal study provides a glimpse of changes in the household involvement of older men over a decade (Keith, 1985b). Observations from 1,332 older men indicated that their participation in housework at two periods of time varied considerably by type of activity. Masculine tasks reflected in household repairs and lawn work were performed by most men at both times. With the exception of increased participation in gardening, most increments in involvement when the men were older occurred in more feminine activities. Indeed, increases in the traditionally feminine activities were striking until frequency of participation was investigated. The majority of wives in these older families, like their younger counterparts, did not receive sustained help.

Expectations for Gender Roles in Older Families. In older families, Brubaker (1985) found that both husbands and wives expected a traditional division of household responsibilities, but they also anticipated that many of those activities would be shared, especially the feminine tasks. In a comparison of dual-earner and dual-retired couples, both types of families reported a traditional division of labor (Brubaker & Hennon, 1982). The wives in the dual-earner families, however, expected to share more responsibilities with their husbands once they were retired. Retired wives also observed that they expected retired women to share more responsibilities with their husbands than what actually was the case in their own household.

In research on expectations for household responsibilities, respondents anticipated that household tasks would be divided in a traditional manner by middle-aged couples and that such a division would continue into old age (Dobson, 1983). It is interesting to note, however, that some responsibilities assigned to middle-aged men were no longer expected of men in older couples. This may have suggested an expectation of contracting roles for these elderly husbands.

Gender-Role Orientation and Behavior in the Household. A continuing question is whether or how orientation toward masculine or feminine characteristics and gender-role ideology interface with actual behavior in the household. There is evidence to suggest that gender-role orientation is associated with the division of work in the household (Huber & Spitze, 1983; Kamo, 1988). In their sample of young adult couples, Nyquist et al. (1985) found that men who scored high on indices of expressiveness that were related to femininity were more likely to help their wives in traditional household tasks. Yet, others have failed to find a connection between egalitarian attitudes toward roles in the family and the subsequent division of labor (Crouter et al., 1987; Ferree, 1988) or beliefs of husbands have been found to be stronger predictors of actual practices than are those of wives (Hiller & Philliber, 1986). Even so, gender-role behavior in the family does not seem to have changed at the same rate as the normative changes (Szinovacz, 1989).

Employment Outside the Home and Gender Roles in the Family. Change in roles such as employment, launching children, and retirement may alter the dynamics of couple interaction and influence the allocation of household tasks (Keith, Dobson, Goudy & Powers, 1981; Kremer, 1985; Szinovacz, 1989). In research on the household division of labor among younger couples, a key question has been about the effect of wives' employment on the husbands' involvement in the family as well as their own participation (Huber & Spitze, 1983; Thompson & Walker, 1989). In contrast, for the older family, the issue is the effect of the retirement of one or both spouses on their engagement in the household. Szinovacz (1989) demonstrates how role theory may be used to think about the impact of retirement on activities in the household. The perspective also may provide a conceptual framework within which to view the consequences of both accumulating and relinquishing roles. Observing that individuals' conceptions of themselves evolve from their involvement in roles, she notes that occupational roles form a part of the role repertoire of the family. Although Szinovacz described how ceasing employment might evoke a redefinition of marital roles involving both spouses, beginning or changing occupational roles in earlier family stages may result in a similar review and adjustment of activities by spouses.

If there is a transition in household roles that occurs with changes in employment status, then not only should the employment status of spouses in younger families have consequences for the allocation of tasks, but the patterns of activities performed in older families also should be responsive to retirement and employment. Therefore, it follows from the reciprocal nature of the marital relationship that the employment status of one spouse may influence and have implications for the involvement of the other in the household.

In general in younger families, the fact that women are employed or the characteristics of their employment (e.g., hours per week spent in work) seem to have little influence on the amount of housework undertaken by husbands (Berk, 1985; Crouter et al., 1987; Pleck, 1985). When husbands in younger families increase their time in family work in response to wives' employment, they often allocate more time to children (Crouter et al., 1987; Pleck, 1985). Wives, however, prefer that husbands increase their efforts in household tasks rather than in childcare (Benin & Agostinelli, 1988). Employment reduces the amount of time women spend on both housework and with children (Berardo et al., 1987). Relative to men in single-earner families, husbands of employed women spend relatively more time in housework, but only because women engaged in paid work do less than full-time homemakers (Berardo et al., 1987).

In the older family, however, the employment status of both spouses was found to influence the engagement of the husband in the household (Keith, Powers & Goudy, 1981). Employed older men participated less in both masculine and feminine tasks than did their retired or partially retired male peers. Moreover, wives' employment seemed to prompt involvement of older men in both masculine and feminine tasks.

At retirement some men view the household as a place where they may reengage in socially acceptable tasks (Crawford, 1971). Early research suggested that men increased their activity in the household at retirement (Ballweg, 1967; Lipman, 1960) whereas, correspondingly, wives of retired men decreased their involvement (Ballweg, 1967). Even though retired men had full responsibility for more tasks than the employed, wives continued to perform exclusively those activities that are usually identified as more feminine (e.g., laundry and ironing). Earlier research suggested that if the involvement of men were influenced by retirement, they were more likely to increase participation in feminine activities inside the household and perhaps those requiring fewer skills. Much research supports the continued gender-typed nature of household activities in older families, despite employment status, after retirement, and even among the unmarried aged (Ade-Ridder & Brubaker, 1988; Dorfman & Heckert, 1988; Keith, 1980; Keith, 1985b). Even so, it has been concluded that older and/or retired men allocate more time to and do a greater share of household work than younger and/or employed men (Szinovacz, 1989).

Dual-retired couples, who might be expected to be the most modern, made few changes in their traditional division of labor when they ceased employment (Brubaker & Hennon, 1982). Studies of retired teachers and their spouses (Keating & Cole, 1980) and of retired women and their husbands (Szinovacz, 1980) found that female retirement altered the division of labor very little. Indeed, participation of some wives actually increased following retirement (Szinovacz, 1989). Thus, despite the fact that couples expect to share more in retirement, especially feminine tasks, most make few changes.

Housework and Well-Being

Does involvement in housework affect well-being? At least two perspectives on the psychological outcomes of involvement in the household by older couples are informative. One view, albeit the one with perhaps the least support, suggests that participation in the household may be stressful, especially for husbands. Early research suggested that participation in feminine tasks might diminish the self-esteem of men (Burke & Weir, 1976), whereas continued gender-typed behavior seemed to facilitate adaptation in old age (Ballweg, 1967). Lipman (1961), however, observed that men who continued to view themselves as good economic providers had lower morale than those who interpreted their marital role as expressive. Increased household involvement by older men may be interpreted as intrusion into the wife's arena and may increase conflict or otherwise disrupt the family (Crawford, 1971; Keating & Cole, 1980; Szinovacz, 1983). Younger women also may be hesitant to relinquish some of their tasks. Earlier, in chapter 3, we observed that women more than men worried that others might not complete tasks in the household as well as they. Research, however, suggests that women more than men may be disadvantaged by their involvement in housework. Research focusing primarily on younger employed spouses generally has indicated that high levels of family work are associated with diminished well-being among women, but increased participation in housework by men did not prompt psychological distress or depressive symptoms (Kessler & McRae, 1982; Ross, Mirowsky & Huber, 1983) and actually may aid the adjustment of men in the family and promote their overall well-being (Pleck, 1983). Husbands in marriages in which housework was divided equally enjoyed greater satisfaction with the division of labor (Benin & Agostinelli, 1988). Women were happier when husbands shared some of the traditional feminine tasks rather than achieving an equal amount of input by doing primarily child care. With increased participation of older men in the household, their satisfaction may be greater (Keith et al., 1981).

The notion that older wives may find involvement of their husbands intrusive suggests that women may be disadvantaged by less gender-typed behavior in the household. The outcomes of shared housework for women may be associated with the family life stage because younger wives beset by more role overload may actually welcome assistance, whereas older women, perhaps with more time to allocate to housework, may prefer to maintain the division of labor as it was earlier. There is some evidence that wives adapt their routines to correspond to those of their retired spouses and that neglecting to do so may negatively affect both spouses (Szinovacz, 1989). Kremer (1985), however, observed that only about 11 percent of retired men believed their wives were disturbed, angry, or dissatisfied with their spending more time at home. In other instances, of course, shared housework in the older family may be prompted by health difficulties that in themselves are likely to be distressing.

Furthermore, whether the husband's involvement is interpreted negatively may vary by social class. Lower-class wives tended to view husbands' increased involvement in the household as interference and were more dissatisfied with their performance, whereas in middle-class families and those with retired wives participation of husbands was more accepted even though partners may have disagreed about the performance of tasks (Szinovacz, 1983).

A second view is that less gender typing in household activities is indicative of a more egalitarian and flexible relationship and should be associated with better mental health for both husbands and wives. Earlier research provided partial support for this perspective among older spouses. Kerckhoff (1966) observed that greater male participation in household tasks fostered higher morale for both spouses whereas a decrease in gender-typed behavior and a more egalitarian division of labor were associated with greater happiness (Clark & Anderson, 1967). Other research found that household involvement was not stressful for older men although benefits derived from participation varied somewhat by the type of task (Keith et al., 1981). Involvement of older men in both masculine and feminine tasks, for example, was linked with greater life satisfaction, but only participation in masculine activities also prompted higher self-esteem. Both masculine and feminine tasks facilitated adjustment to retirement for the fully retired but not for the partially retired.

For the most part, the outcomes of cross-gender behavior for men have been found to be either mostly positive or neutral. It is tempting to conclude that the benefits derived by men who behaved less traditionally and involved themselves more fully in the household to some degree support the perspective that androgynous behavior may increase adaptability and may be helpful in adjusting to late-life transitions such as retirement. Masculine activities, however, were linked to a greater number of positive outcomes for men than was involvement in feminine tasks, although participation in the latter did not have a negative effect (Keith et al., 1981).

In summary, at least younger women seem to be disadvantaged in terms of mental health when they are highly involved in more traditional family work, whereas men are not similarly jeopardized and may actually benefit (Pleck, 1983). Younger women, though, may derive benefits from their husbands' participation in the home. A low level of family work by husbands in two-job families was associated with role overload among wives and was accompanied by diminished psychological well-being (Pleck, 1983). Furthermore, benefits of husbands' involvement in the household may extend to wives who are not employed outside the home. Receiving help from husbands in the household decreased depression of their wives whether or not the latter were employed (Ross et al., 1983). In contrast, involvement of older husbands, while having slightly positive or neutral effects for them, may foster some discomfort for their wives (Keith & Schafer, 1986).

In the presentation of research that follows, we identify how several aspects of gender roles in families varied across the life stages and between husbands and wives, with special attention to the older family. We begin by describing the attitudinal context from which the families operated as reflected in beliefs about the division of labor within and outside the household. We then consider whether processes within the family and responses to them (e.g., disagreement, satisfaction with activities, role strain, and evaluations of performance) varied over the life stages and the extent to which they were experienced differently by husbands and wives. Differential involvement in masculine and feminine tasks by younger and older spouses and the factors prompting these activities were investigated. In a further analysis, involvement in masculine and feminine tasks by both spouses was examined in relation to psychological well-being.

INSIGHTS INTO GENDER ROLES OF COUPLES ACROSS THE LIFE STAGES

In this section of the chapter, using information from our sample of 336 couples, we address our guiding questions, which were: (1) Did spouses hold comparable conceptions of gender roles across the life stages? (2) What were the perceptions of husbands and wives of their work-family life? (3) How did involvement of spouses in the household vary by gender and life stage, and which personal characteristics fostered participation? and (4) What were the implications of gender role behavior and attitudes for psychological well-being?

Gender-Role Attitudes

Did conceptions of appropriate gender-role behavior vary over stages of the life course, and if so, how did they differ? To obtain insight into these issues, we conducted separate one-way analyses of variance for men and women in the four life-stage groups.

Two indices were used to assess views of gender roles. One measure asked couples who should have most responsibility for cooking and housekeeping and for the provider role (Husband always—wife always). The second measure asked about attitudes toward employment of women outside the home and its potential for interference with family life (see chapter 2 for a more detailed wording of both indices).

Older and younger families clearly held different conceptions of appropriate behavior for males and females in the household and in the workplace (Table 5.1). Usually older women, compared to those who were younger, were especially traditional in their expectations for acceptance of responsibility in the household and in employment. Among men, however, those who were middle-aged and older were similar in their assessments of norms for gender roles in the household and were more traditional than the two youngest groups. But the oldest men were differentiated from all other men in their opinions about the effect of women's employment on the family. They were more likely to believe that women should not work outside the home and that the emotional life of the family suffers when women have full-time employment.

Table 5.1
Gender-Role Attitudes, Household Involvement, and Personal Characteristics by Family Life Stages (One-way Analyses of Variance)

	F Values	
	Husbands N = 336	Wives N = 336
Interpersonal and psychological characteristics		
Disagreement	6.84*** (1,2/3,4)	12.49*** (1,2/3,4)
Evaluation of performance	3.81** (4/1,2)	3.83** (4/1,3;2/1)
Depressive symptoms	.31	.30
Satisfaction	1.37	1.56
Household involvement		
Feminine tasks	5.32*** (1,2,3/4)	10.22*** (1,2,3/4;3/1)
Masculine tasks	2.63* (1/2,3)	8.26*** (2,3,4/1)
Gender-role attitudes		
Gender-role attitudes	3.68** (3,4/1)	9.81*** (4/1,2,3;3/1)
Attitudes toward roles of women	11.73*** (4/1,2,3;3/1)	7.03*** (4/1,2)

Numbers in parentheses refer to life-cycle groups; 1 is youngest, 4 oldest. Numbers to the left of the "/" sign indicate groups significantly more negative in response to work-family variables, less involved in the household, and holding more-traditional gender-role attitudes.

  * $p < .05$
 ** $p < .01$
*** $p < .001$

Responses to Work and Family by Life Stage

Within families outcomes such as disagreement, evaluations of their behavior, and amount of role strain suggested that the atmosphere in them varied a great deal depending on the life-cycle stage (Table 5.1). Families with children in the home, the two youngest groups, had relationships characterized by more disagreement and greater role strain.

Table 5.2
Views of Husbands and Wives by Family Life Stages (Paired t Values)

	Couples			
	Stage 1 N = 85	Stage 2 N = 88	Stage 3 N = 81	Stage 4 N = 82
Evaluation of performance	3.86***	2.81***	4.31***	4.11***
Disagreement	.31	.46	.11	1.76*
Satisfaction	1.27	.78	.55	3.47***
Role strain	5.37***	6.89***	5.25***	4.08***
Depressive symptoms	5.13***	4.05***	4.18***	4.39***
Gender-role attitudes	1.18	.53	.97	.93
Attitudes toward roles of women	1.69*	2.78***	.44	3.05***

  * p <.10
 ** p <.05
*** p <.01

That is, younger spouses felt that job and family demands might interfere with one another, that the sheer amount of work interfered with how well they were able to complete it, or that others would not be able to do household tasks as well as they. Despite their worries about getting things done, younger persons evaluated their performance in the household more positively than the oldest men and women, who tended to devalue the quality of their work in the family more than most other age groups. Even though concerns of families differed by life stage, satisfaction derived from work-family tasks and depressive symptoms were comparable across the age groups.

Preferences and Perceptions of Husbands and Wives

Did these husbands and wives share views and preferences for gender roles? Did they have common observations of processes in their families and did congruency in perceptions vary over the life stages? Paired t-tests were employed to compare husbands' and wives' views of gender roles and assessments of family processes (Table 5.2).

Regardless of their life stage, wives consistently assessed their performance in work-family tasks more positively than did husbands. Despite their more favorable evaluations of performance, however, women experienced significantly greater role strain than their husbands. That is, attaining better role performance may have been accomplished at the expense of greater strain.

Except for the middle-aged, wives held more modern views of roles of women than those of their spouses. Finally, the oldest men reported greater disagreement in the family than was observed by their wives, and they expressed more dissatisfaction with work-family roles. The greatest discrepancies in perceptions were among the oldest husbands and wives. The oldest husbands and wives had similar views on only one of the seven indices compared to agreement on three or four by partners in the other age groups. There was only one area in which husbands and wives were in agreement regardless of life-cycle stage; this was in their assessments of who should have more responsibility for work-family tasks, i.e., one of the two measures of gender-role attitudes.

Extent of Involvement in the Household

The oldest men were distinguished from males of other ages by their significantly greater involvement in feminine tasks in the household (e.g., laundry, dishwashing) (Table 5.1). Corresponding to their husbands' greater participation in feminine tasks, older women usually were less involved in traditionally feminine tasks than were middle-aged and younger women. Younger women allocated substantially more of their time to these activities than the middle-aged and older women. Thus, with age these husbands performed more feminine tasks in the household whereas wives spent less time on them. Overall, life stage made more difference in the involvement of women in these tasks than for men, probably reflecting the demands of children for the youngest women and the outcomes of retirement for the oldest men.

Participation in masculine tasks around the house was also age-linked, with youngest men less involved in masculine activities than the two middle groups of men. Using the two indicators of home repairs and yard work, the participation of older men was not differentiated from that of any other group of men.

Involvement in masculine activities especially varied by life stage among women. Older women were less active in masculine tasks than all three groups of younger women. The youngest women were significantly more involved in cross-gender activities than all of their older counterparts. But these same young women were engaged in traditional feminine activities as well.

Correlates of Masculine/Feminine Involvement in the Household

What factors predicted the extent of involvement in masculine and feminine tasks in the household? Were they the same for husbands and wives? To answer these questions, demographic characteristics (education, family income, employment status of both spouses) and gender-role attitudes were considered in relation to involvement. Multiple-regression analyses were used to determine the relative importance of demographic characteristics and attitudes toward gender roles in predicting masculine and feminine involvement in the household (Table 5.3). Because there was little difference by life stage in the factors that influenced involvement in the household among men, the two groups of younger men were combined, as were the middle-aged and older groups. Separate analyses were performed for younger and older men. To conserve space where possible we present results from the combined groups. Important differences in gender-role involvement by age that were obscured by combining life-stage categories are noted. Because there was more variability in the predictors by life stage among women, analyses were completed separately for the four life-stage groups of women.

Involvement in Feminine Activities. Regression models for involvement in feminine tasks included education, family income, employment status of husbands and wives, and preferences for gender roles in the family. Employment status of husbands was used only in analyses for the two older groups because almost all of the younger men were employed at the time of the research.

Following Ross et al. (1983), the measure of feminine activities reported here in most detail assessed who usually did the cooking and housekeeping (except cooking and childcare). Both of these involve tasks with recurrent and routine demands and perhaps less flexibility in scheduling than some other household and family work. Response categories included "Husband always" (1) to "Wife always" (5). These two items were summed with a higher score reflecting a more traditional distribution of housework.

A second set of measures assessed and summed participation in the feminine tasks of laundry, grocery shopping, and dishwashing. Differing from those used before, response categories ranged from "Spouse always does most" (1) to "Self does most" (5). A high score reflected greater involvement in the tasks. Only the first measure of participation in feminine tasks is reported in the tables.

Involvement in feminine tasks among men from youth to middle age was strongly influenced by their ideas of the appropriate division of labor in the household ($r = .63$; $r = .38$) (Table 5.3).

Table 5.3
Involvement in Feminine and Masculine Tasks by Wives and Husbands by Life Stages (Multiple Regression Analyses)

	Wives								Husbands			
	Stage 1		Stage 2		Stage 3		Stage 4		Stages 1 & 2		Stages 3 & 4	
	r	B	r	B	r	B	r	B	r	B	r	B
Feminine Tasks												
Gender-role attitudes	.53	.49**	.62	.55**	.65	.60**	.01	.01	.63	.60**	.38	.38**
Education	-.19	-.04	-.21	-.11	-.29	-.09	.26	.22**	-.03	-.18	-.06	-.08
Income	-.22	-.05	.08	.04	-.01	.17*	.17	.01	-.05	.10	.07	.09
Wife's employment	.26	.01	.44	.23**	.35	.21**	-.05	-.02	.33	.12	.09	.07
Husband's employment					-.03	-.13	-.22	-.18			-.09	-.15
R^2	.28		.46		.50		.10		.42		.18	
Masculine Tasks												
Gender-role attitudes	-.22	-.29**	-.29	-.38**	.25	.38**	.09	.05	.02	.08	-.12	-.08
Education	.08	.07	.06	-.04	.07	.21	-.08	-.13	-.06	-.09	.00	.05
Income	.07	-.04	-.07	-.17	.17	.34*	.07	.02	.09	.12	-.08	-.17
Wife's employment	-.01	.13	-.01	-.08	.24	.25**	-.13	-.14	-.15	-.18**	-.20	-.24**
Husband's employment					.06	.05	-.26	-.26*			.02	.06
R^2	.07		.12		.23		.10		.05		.07	

* $p < .10$
** $p < .05$

In general, men with nontraditional attitudes were more involved in feminine tasks. An exception was that participation in feminine tasks by the oldest men was independent of their ideas about gender roles ($r = .00$). The amount of variance explained in feminine involvement by men varied from 42 percent for the two groups of younger men to 18 percent for those who were older. Younger men with employed wives participated somewhat more in feminine tasks ($r = .33$), but wives' employment status did not have a significant effect when other factors were considered. The involvement of middle-aged and older men was not affected by their wives' employment.

Models identical to those for men were considered for the four separate life-stage groups of women (Table 5.3). Among all but the oldest women, preferences for gender roles were strong determinants of the division of labor in their households. Women who embraced traditional expectations for gender roles were most involved in feminine tasks. The correlations between attitudes toward gender roles and involvement in feminine tasks ranged from $r = .53$ for the youngest women, to $r = .62$ and $r = .65$ for the next two groups. Participation in feminine tasks was completely independent of gender role attitudes among the oldest women ($r = .01$) and was a marked contrast to those in the other life stages.

Among the youngest women with children under age 6, being a full-time homemaker was associated with more involvement in feminine tasks ($r = .26$), but it did not have a significant effect when other factors were included in the model. The employment status of women with school-age children and of women whose children had left the home most recently was linked to their involvement in the household ($r = .44$ and $r = .35$, respectively). Although employment status was significant in the multivariate model, it figured less importantly in involvement in feminine tasks than did their attitudes toward gender roles. Employment diminished involvement in homemaking tasks for these women.

Although the model accounted for much less variance in involvement of the oldest women, a higher level of education contributed to their greater participation in the household ($r = .26$). Husbands' retirement was correlated with less involvement in feminine tasks by the oldest women ($r = -.22$), but it was not significant in the regression model. Regardless of their age, women's responsibility for these feminine tasks was independent of their family income. As in the instance of men, the model explained substantially more variance in involvement of the younger women than of their older counterparts.

Additional analyses of feminine tasks were done in which laundry, grocery shopping, and dishwashing were considered as a group of tasks. In these analyses the two youngest groups were combined, as were the two oldest groups. Demographic characteristics as well as beliefs about appropriate gender-role behavior were included in separate regression analyses for men and women.

Again, attitudes toward gender roles were the strongest predictors of involvement in feminine activities for younger and older men ($r = .42$ and $r = .27$, respectively; $R^2 = 19$ and 17 percent, respectively) and for younger women ($r = .40$; $R^2 = 17$ percent). Educational level was the most important factor in determining involvement of the two oldest groups of women ($r = .26$, $R^2 = 14$ percent). Education among the older men also was important ($r = .21$). In these older families better-educated spouses maintained a traditional division of labor in which the wife was most involved in feminine tasks (i.e., dishwashing, grocery shopping, and laundry). For most families, expectations about who should have responsibility for work-family activities were more important determinants of the actual division of labor than attitudes toward employment and family roles of women or the social status characteristics of the family. For many, then, their gender-role attitudes were put into practice in the household.

Involvement in Masculine Activities. In general, for both men and women, the variables were poorer predictors of participation in masculine than feminine tasks. Among the two groups of men, only 5 to 7 percent of the variance in masculine activities was accounted for (Table 5.3). Only the employment status of the wife was important in determining involvement in masculine activities around the house by men. Both younger and older men whose wives were employed outside the home were more involved in masculine tasks ($r = -.15$, younger men; $r = -.17$, older men).

Again, analyses for women are reported for the four separate groups (Table 5.3). Involvement in masculine tasks was prompted by holding nontraditional beliefs except among the two younger groups of women ($r = -.22$ and $r = .29$, respectively). But among women whose children had left the home most recently, traditional attitudes ($r = .25$), being a full-time homemaker ($r = .24$), and having a higher family income ($r = .17$) fostered greater involvement in masculine tasks.

For these oldest women, their husbands' employment status was more important than their own in determining their household involvement, in contrast to that of middle-aged women. Retirement of the oldest husbands diminished their wives' participation in masculine activities. In addition to the effect of nontraditional expectations, being a homemaker was linked with performing more masculine tasks by middle-aged women.

Next we consider whether participation in masculine and feminine activities had a differential influence on psychological well-being, as indicated by depressive symptoms. Did greater involvement in either masculine or feminine household tasks foster mental health, or was such participation benign?

Masculine and Feminine Involvement and Depressive Symptoms

In this section our primary concern is whether the type of household task may be a part of the conditions in which depressive symptoms are fostered. Was participation in masculine or feminine activities in the home especially troublesome for husbands or wives, for the young or the old?

Using separate multiple regression models for men and women in each life-cycle group, the effects of family income, education, employment status, and involvement in masculine and feminine activities in the household on depressive symptoms were examined. In a second set of models, spouse's education, employment status, and participation in housework were considered in relation to depressive symptoms of the other partner.

When respondents' own characteristics rather than those of their spouses were used to predict their well-being, housework was more salient to depressive symptoms of women than of men. Participation in feminine activities had no effect on distress among men. Involvement in masculine activities, however, influenced distress among the youngest and oldest groups, although the direction of the effects was reversed. Older men experienced fewer depressive symptoms if they were more involved in masculine tasks ($r = -.29$). Wives of the youngest men benefited most if they were more involved themselves in masculine tasks ($r = -.25$). Women with children older than 6 years and the oldest women both were less depressed if they were more involved in feminine tasks ($r = -.41$ and $r = -.28$, respectively). Distress reported by middle-aged women was independent of either type of task; rather, they enjoyed less well-being when their husbands were unemployed ($r = .18$) whereas their own employment status had little salience for their mental health.

Among the four age groups of men, from youngest to oldest, the models accounted for .11, .15, .05, and .10 percent of the variance in depressive symptoms respectively. Among women the percentage of explained variance in depressive symptoms was .20, .34, .10, and .14 for each of the four age groups respectively.

Although the variables studied were not very good predictors of depressive symptoms, one difference between the models for the age groups warrants comment. The effects of one spouse's household involvement on the well-being of the other were markedly different in significant ways for older and younger couples. Older husbands had more depressive symptoms if their wives were highly involved in masculine tasks ($r = .30$) whereas their wives were distressed when their spouses participated more in feminine activities ($r = .27$). Negative effects of cross-gender participation were not observed in any of the other age groups.

Not only did the oldest spouses benefit from high involvement in gender-typed activities, but they were disadvantaged by their spouses' cross-gender participation. This was especially highlighted for older women in an investigation of the importance of disagreement over work-family roles as a possible contributing factor to depressive symptoms. Disagreement between spouses about work-family roles was the most important determinant of depressive symptoms for all age and gender groups except older women, for whom a nontraditional division of labor was most troublesome (Keith & Schafer, 1986).

What seemed to prompt disagreement between spouses and was the division of labor a factor in conflict within these marriages? A less-traditional division of labor in feminine tasks was costly in terms of disagreement over work-family activities for younger men and women ($r = -.27$ and $r = -.18$) and for older women ($r = -.17$). Indeed, homemakers, who occupied a more traditional role than wives in the labor force, observed less disagreement in their families than did employed women in dual-earner households ($t = 3.17$, $p < .01$). Although the relationship between nontraditional activities and disagreement was not significant among older men ($r = -.18$), it was in the same direction as those for the other age and gender groups (Keith & Schafer, 1986).

SUMMARY

In this chapter we have reviewed some of the literature on gender-role attitudes and behavior over family life stages. Based on previous work of others and our own, a number of questions guided an analysis of gender roles in younger and older families. We considered differences in behavior and attitudes across four family life stages and variation in the views of husbands and wives in each stage. Did perceptions of appropriate gender roles vary by life stage? To what extent did husbands and wives share views of gender roles? What were the consequences for mental health of holding traditional or nontraditional views of the roles of men and women for the spouses we studied?

To the extent that preferences for gender roles are realized in actual behavior in the family—and our evidence suggests they are—life in these younger and older families was somewhat different. Two measures of attitudes toward gender roles were employed. In one measure couples were asked to indicate who (husband or wife) should have more responsibility for activities undertaken within the household and as provider. A second measure dealt with attitudes toward employment of women with young children, the relative salience that marriage and family should have vis-à-vis work and a career for women, and the extent to which the emotional life of the family suffers when wives have full-time employment.

Compared to the oldest couples, husbands and wives in the youngest families held less traditional expectations for and views on the roles of men and women on both indices. Although there was some variation between the family life stages, the youngest and oldest families shared the fewest observations about gender roles.

The youngest spouses had to manage the most disagreement and role strain in their lives. Yet, despite these pressures and worries, they tended to evaluate their performance in work-family activities most positively. In contrast, the oldest men and women most often devalued the quality of their own participation in work-family tasks. Spouses' evaluations of the efforts of their partners, however, were independent of family life stage. Even though spouses may have judged their own performance in work and family activities harshly, their companions did not view them negatively.

The tendency of the oldest group to denigrate their own performance may have been, in part, due to the retirement of their spouse rather than their own. Regardless of their own employment status, for example, the oldest spouses, either husbands or wives, with retired partners devalued their own performance. For these older spouses, retirement of a partner was perhaps cause for scrutiny resulting in a negative judgment of their own performance. Retirement may have underscored problems that had not surfaced previously.

Was there less gender typing of activities later in life, as some literature suggests? That is, were older men more involved in feminine activities and older women more active in masculine activities? Older men participated in feminine activities more frequently than middle-aged and younger men and correspondingly their wives were less involved in these tasks. Despite their more traditional attitudes, in carrying out feminine roles, the oldest women were the least traditional, that is, they were less involved than other age groups. But they did not compensate by taking on additional masculine activities.

Younger women maintained more traditional feminine roles than their oldest counterparts. It must not be concluded, however, that the youngest women had young children and were therefore constrained toward femininity by the demands of parenthood (Gutmann, 1975), because these women also engaged most in cross-gender activities, that is, in more masculine tasks. In contrast, the youngest husbands were among those least involved in the household, in both masculine and feminine tasks. Thus, young wives carried a greater load of both types of activities while holding less-traditional expectations, whereas the oldest women were less involved in the traditional feminine tasks while at the same time maintaining the most traditional views of the activities most appropriate for them. Thus, in sharp contrast to that of other couples, involvement in both types of household activities by the oldest husbands and wives was independent of gender-role orientation. If gender-role attitudes were a factor in the household participation of the oldest spouses, the effect was indirect.

For whatever reasons, compared to other women, the oldest wives participated least in both feminine and masculine tasks. On the two measures of feminine tasks, retirement of the husband was correlated with less feminine involvement on the part of the wife ($r = -.19$, cooking/housekeeping; $-.24$, shopping, laundry, etc.) although it explained a significant portion of the variance only in the former. Limiting the assessment of masculine tasks to only two was a disadvantage, and respondents may have underestimated their involvement in masculine activities as a whole. On more detailed indices of gender-role orientation and attitudes, older women also might have been less gender typed. Questions about gender roles directed toward later life probably would have been useful. Notwithstanding, these older families were differentiated from some of the other age groups by their patterns of involvement in feminine tasks.

Among the strongest findings were those that linked beliefs about gender roles to actual household involvement. Although this may seem obvious, there is not always a consistent relationship between views of gender roles and behavior (Orlofsky, Cohen & Ramsden, 1985). Conceptualization of appropriate roles for men and women, for the most part, were reflected in the extent of household involvement, especially in feminine tasks by both husbands and wives and in masculine roles by women. Beliefs about appropriate gender roles were least closely associated with performance of tasks among the oldest spouses. Even as husbands became more involved in feminine activities in the household, attitudes toward gender roles endorsed by them and their spouses remained traditional.

To what extent did husbands and wives share views of gender roles? Within the marital dyad, did husbands and wives hold similar views and was there variation across the family life stages?

Regardless of family life stage, husbands and wives did not differ in their perceptions of which spouse should have the most responsibility for tasks inside and outside the family. Except for the middle-aged, however, husbands and wives differed in their views of the role of women in the labor force, with men being consistently more traditional.

Within the marital dyad, the oldest couples tended to be more heterogeneous than the younger partners. On seven assessments, the oldest spouses differed from one another on all but one. In ways, some of the experiences of older men seemed more negative than those of their wives; at least, they constructed their views of dynamics in the family and of their own behavior more bleakly. Whereas other couples, for example, were in agreement about the amount of conflict in their relationships, older men observed more disagreement in their family than did their wives. Older men also were less satisfied with their roles and devalued the quality of their performance. Yet, wives were more depressed and felt considerably more role strain, that is, overload and worry about how well things would be done. The reciprocal aspects of the relationship were highlighted in the instance of role strain of wives. Their role strain was greater if their husbands were dissatisfied with their own roles and when the men felt they performed poorly themselves.

What were the consequences of gender-typed behavior for mental health? Involvement in the household in either masculine or feminine tasks figured more importantly in the well-being of wives than of husbands. In summary, the oldest men had fewer depressive symptoms if they were more involved in masculine tasks around the home ($r = -.29$). The youngest women with children under age 6 benefited from their involvement in masculine tasks ($r = -.25$). This finding about gender-role behavior parallels an observation by Whisman and Jacobson (1989) about a personality characteristic; they noted that low masculinity was associated with depression in women. But in contrast women in our sample with older children and the oldest wives both were less distressed when they had more responsibility for feminine activities ($r = -.41, -.28$ respectively). Thus, for three of the four groups of women, household involvement had implications for psychological well-being, albeit with an inconsistent pattern.

Should we be drawn to recommend an increase in cross-gender involvement in the household as an avenue for engagement by members of the older family, it is important to review our findings. As noted, participation in cross-gender activities did not increase the psychological well-being of these older spouses, and it diminished that of their partners. Beyond this, however, both older husbands and wives experienced positive outcomes from engaging in gender-typed tasks. Yet, we must be cautious in this interpretation and again call attention to the limitations of the measures of masculine and feminine tasks, even though they were fairly representative of some of those commonly employed. These findings contrast with those of Sinnott (1982), who found that androgyny was associated with better mental health, and the observations of Shichman and Cooper (1984) that androgynous persons enjoyed greater life satisfaction. To the extent that involvement in cross-gender activities may indicate more androgynous behavior, it is clear that for these older couples such patterns did not directly benefit the participant and were disadvantageous for their partners. These findings about older couples may be especially important because they also speak to the consequences that gender roles have not only for the individual but also for the partner. But our observations about older couples contrast with those from research on younger families indicating that young women benefit from their spouses' involvement in the household. Once again this calls our attention to the potential differences in characteristics of partners across the life stages and underscores the need to consider both husbands and wives in our studies of older families.

6

Typologies of Marriages: Differences across the Life Stages

In this chapter we use two typologies of marriages to consider further how spousal relationships may vary over the life stages in what seem to be quite different kinds of partnerships. Consideration of correlates of the proposed patterns should give a view of how lives of married couples are constructed across an array of possible relationships.

Economic and social forces jointly influenced the fundamental nature of marriage in the 1980s (Li & Caldwell, 1987). Marriages were changing from those in which only the husband was employed with the wife caring for the house and children, a "complementary" type, to one in which both partners were employed and were responsible for housework, that is, a "parallel" pattern (Ross, Mirowsky & Huber, 1983). These represent traditional and modern marriages, respectively, as defined by Bowen and Orthner (1983). Although the question arises whether marital adjustment is greater in modern or traditional marriages, evidence that either type of partnership is the clear pattern of preferred choice is lacking (Li & Caldwell, 1987). Rather, it has been suggested that extent of agreement or disagreement between couples on gender-role attitudes may be more significant than the particular configuration they maintain. To examine the importance of congruence or incongruence in sex-role ideology for the marital relationship, one of the typologies employs agreement between spouses as a central concept.

The two typologies analyzed in this chapter are (1) contemporary marriage types as proposed by Scanzoni (1980) and later investigated by Quinn and Davidson (1986) and (2) marital sex-role congruence as

suggested and tested by Bowen and Orthner (1983) and discussed by
Bowen (1989).

The first typology is organized around the actual division of labor by
focusing on the employment status of the wife and the extent to which
financial responsibility for the family is shared by the spouses. The
second typology focuses on the ideological environment of the family,
namely the extent to which perspectives on gender roles held by spouses
are modern or traditional and whether they are shared by the partners.
We first investigate attributes of spouses and families that characterize
and differentiate between types of contemporary marriages that have
been identified in the literature (Scanzoni, 1980). Next, profiles of family
characteristics associated with ideologically congruent and incongruent
marital relationships are developed.

CONTEMPORARY MARRIAGE TYPES

Scanzoni (1980) proposed that contemporary marriages may be categorized into at least three types: (1) equal partner, (2) senior-junior partner, and (3) head-complement patterns. These types represent varying
structures and marital role relationships ranging from egalitarian to traditional ways of relating to one another. The equal-partner pattern represents the most modern form for marriage whereas the junior partner
and head-complement types reflect more traditional spousal
relationships.

These patterns indicate variability in configurations that the family
may take. In the equal-partner pattern, spouses are symmetrically responsible for household economic provision and are therefore coproviders (Scanzoni, 1980). In this pattern, spouses will be involved in dual
careers in which both have full occupational involvement and advancement in work while assuming responsibility for providing economically
for the household. In identifying couples in this pattern, determining
factors are not only employment of the wife outside the home but also
the belief that she shares equally in providing for the family financially.
It is critical to the definition of the equal-partner pattern that employed
women view themselves as coproviders and that they see their work as
having consequences on a par with that of their husbands with regard
to financial provision for well-being of the family (Scanzoni, 1980).

In the equal-partner situation, in which both spouses have responsibility for finances, power is most equally divided, and gender roles
are the most flexible and relaxed. Presumably it is the pattern that would
be most responsive to individual preferences. Scanzoni suggested that
this pattern may be the most satisfying marital relationship.

Wives in the junior-partner pattern define their employment as secondary to that of their husbands. In doing so, they attribute greater

consequences to their spouses' occupational involvement for the economic welfare of the household. In the head-complement types of relationships the husband has complete responsibility for earning family income, and the wife is not employed outside the home. Role relationships between spouses in these work-family patterns are thought to be the most traditional.

Scanzoni (1980) found that women in equal-partner marriages were more occupationally committed than were junior partners, who in turn were more committed than wives who were complements to their husbands. Men and women in equal partnerships also had higher family incomes than the other patterns. Furthermore, men in equal-partner relationships were more involved in household tasks than those in other types of families and in turn their wives more often performed tasks such as repairs that are often completed by men. Equal-partner families also held more egalitarian notions of the roles of husbands and wives than spouses in the other patterns.

Quinn and Davidson (1986) studied self-esteem as an individual psychological characteristic that might vary across the types. Power in the family was examined to determine if decision making would be reflected in shifts in spousal influence across the patterns. They also investigated communication effectiveness, intimacy, and equity in relation to the types of marriages. A dominant assumption is that in equal-partner marriages, compared to the other types, communication would be more effective, and there would be greater intimacy, higher esteem, a more equal distribution of power, and greater equity (Quinn & Davidson, 1986). Whereas Scanzoni observed relationships between the marital types and the division of labor, commitment to work, and gender role orientations, Quinn and Davidson, using analysis-of-variance procedures, did not find significant differences between the marital types on communication, power, intimacy, self-esteem, equity, or marital adjustment.

In this research we raise several questions and extend the work of Scanzoni and of Quinn and Davidson by addressing spousal well-being in the three patterns in multivariate analyses. Did husbands and wives fare better psychologically in some patterns than in others? Did they report fewer depressive symptoms in some patterns than others? Was it easier to maintain higher self-regard in some patterns? Were some patterns more conducive to amicable relations, with less disagreement between spouses? Did husbands and wives find greater satisfaction with their roles in some marriage patterns rather than others? Or were psychological well-being and responses to work-family roles largely independent of the type of marriage? Finally, were the profiles of the marriage types different for older and younger families?

We studied both men and women of various ages, whereas Scanzoni considered only younger women. Scanzoni did not use multivariate procedures and investigated material resources, involvement in house-hold tasks, and preferences for gender roles of husbands and wives separately in relation to each of the patterns. We develop profiles of the three patterns by considering several characteristics of spouses and their relationships simultaneously as well as separately.

Development of the Typology

Following Scanzoni, three patterns were derived by assessing the employment status of both spouses and the extent to which responsibility for providing income for the family was shared. The equal-partner pattern included spouses who were both employed and who indicated they had equal responsibility for providing financially for their family; 14 percent of the spouses had this type of marriage. The junior-partner relationship was comprised of couples who were both employed but in which the husband assumed primary financial responsibility for the household; 37 percent of the families were in this pattern. The head-complement pattern included families in which the husband was employed and the wife was a full-time homemaker; 49 percent of the families comprised this pattern.

Marriage Types and Family Life Stages

The frequency of couples in the marriage patterns varied somewhat across the family life stages. In this analysis, the two youngest groups of couples were combined as were the two oldest. About equal proportions of the younger (50 percent) and older couples (47 percent) were in the pattern which Scanzoni described as the head-complement relationship with the husband as head of the family and the wife not employed outside the home. More than one-third of the younger families (39 percent) and 34 percent of the middle-aged and older families were located in the junior-partner pattern, in which the wife was employed but the husband had primary financial responsibility for the family. Spouses were equal partners, with both employed and sharing equal responsibility for the family finances, in the remaining 11 percent of the younger families and 20 percent of the older families. Although both spouses in younger families more often were employed, relationships were less likely to reflect equal-partner patterns than were those of middle-aged and older persons. With children no longer in the home, women may have viewed their contributions to family finances as equivalent to those of their spouses, whether through their provisions for college expenses for older children or savings as the family drew nearer to retirement. In older couples, perhaps, wives may have continued employment following their spouses' retirement and assumed increased responsibility for maintenance of the family. Or if husbands were retired and wives remained in the labor force, they may have viewed their financial responsibility as at least on a par with that of their spouse. Now we can ask which, if any, factors differentiated these patterns and whether they were comparable across age groups.

Marriage Types and Personal Characteristics

Initially, one-way analyses of variance were performed to determine which factors were differentially associated with the three marriage types among younger and older husbands and wives. The two youngest groups of couples (i.e., those with children in the home) were combined, as were the two older groups. Separate analyses of the three marriage types were conducted for the four life stage groups by sex (i.e., young husbands, young wives, and middle-aged and older husbands and wives).

Extending the work of Scanzoni (1980) and Quinn and Davidson (1986), we examined the responses of husbands and wives to roles within the household relative to the amount of disagreement and satisfaction derived from participation in work-family tasks. Assessments of well-being were reflected in self-concept and depressive symptoms. Finally, perspectives of spouses on gender roles in the family were assessed in two ways: attitudes toward roles of women and actual behavior represented by involvement in cooking and housekeeping. Attitudes toward gender roles focused especially on employment activities of women and the potential for interference between work and family. Spouses, for example, indicated whether they agreed or disagreed with the following statements: "Women with young children should not work outside the home." "For a woman, marriage and family should be more important than work and a career." "All in all, the emotional life of a family suffers when the woman has a full-time job or career." Responses to work-family relationships were assessed by disagreement between spouses and the satisfaction obtained from work-family activities.

Disagreement. The univariate analyses indicated that disagreement between spouses was associated with the three types of marriages for all of the life-stage and gender groups (F = 9.60, $p < .001$, F = 3.70, $p < .05$, young husbands and wives, respectively; F = 3.81, $p < .05$, and F = 4.04, $p < .05$, older husbands and wives, respectively). Across the life stages, there was more disagreement in the egalitarian families regardless of age and the least in the most traditional households in which wives were not employed. Therefore, the traditional pattern was more conducive to amicable relations for these spouses.

Satisfaction. Satisfaction derived from work-family activities was not linked with patterns except among young wives (F = 5.82, $p < .01$).

Younger women in the egalitarian and junior-partner patterns were more dissatisfied than women who were not employed and had no responsibility for family finances. For most of these partners, however, the type of marriage made little difference in the satisfaction they obtained from their work-family activities.

Mental Health. Did some patterns foster better mental health than others? No, they did not for the couples in this sample. At least as reflected in observations about self-concept and depressive symptoms, no single pattern either promoted or eroded the individual well-being of these partners. Thus, for these spouses equal partnerships were not more positive for mental health, as suggested by Scanzoni (1980). Rather, our results support those of Quinn and Davidson (1986), who observed that marital sex-role congruence did not ensure improved mental health.

Gender Roles. In the univariate analyses, gender roles both as practiced in the family and attitudes toward them differentiated between marriage patterns. Across the age groups, involvement by men in feminine work in the household was greatest in the egalitarian families and least in the head-complement pattern in which wives were not employed ($F = 17.52$, $p < .001$; $F = 3.75$, $p < .05$, younger and older men). In general, the amount of feminine household involvement of husbands and wives in the junior-partner pattern was located between and was significantly different from the extent of participation in female tasks by spouses in both of other patterns.

Involvement in male household activities was also associated with the types of marriage. Older men in the head-complement pattern, in which their wives were not employed, engaged more frequently in masculine activities ($F = 6.84$, $p < .001$), whereas older women in the equal-partner relationship spent less time on masculine activities than their peers in the other two types of marriages ($F = 4.90$, $p < .01$).

Attitudes toward gender roles followed much the same trend, with the most modern views of relationships between spouses found in the egalitarian households, followed by the junior-partner and head-complement patterns. Members of families in which the wife was not employed outside the home and in which she was not responsible for contributing to finances had significantly more traditional and restricted views of the roles of women.

Multivariate Analyses of Marriage Types

Discriminant analyses were used to assess which, if any, of several personal characteristics presented earlier best differentiated among the three marriage types. By using this technique, it was possible to consider a categorical variable such as the three types of marriages in relation to other categorical and/or continuous variables simultaneously. The standardized partial-regression coefficients are comparable to those yielded by a conventional multiple-regression analysis. The analyses will permit us to observe not only which, if any, characteristics differentiate among the three types of marriages but also the nature of the distinction between categories, that is, which profiles of the marriage types are most similar or different. In this kind of analysis, the size of the coefficients for the personal characteristics indicate the relative discriminating power of each when other dimensions are also specified in the same model. These analyses should provide a profile of characteristics of families in the patterns. In previous research that investigated the marriage types, univariate analyses of variance were most often used. In this analysis, the following characteristics were considered in relation to the three marriage types: education, income, disagreement between spouses over work-family roles, satisfaction with work-family tasks, involvement in masculine and feminine tasks in the household, self-concept, depressive symptoms, and attitudes toward gender roles.

In the discriminant analyses there was one significant function for each of the four age and gender groups tested (Table 6.1). The most important factors in differentiating the marital patterns were the distribution of housework and attitudes toward gender roles. The salience of these characteristics was observed regardless of place in the family life stage. Spouses who were equal partners in employment and in finances shared significantly more housework and held the most liberal gender-role attitudes. The junior-partner couples, however, generally maintained more nontraditional attitudes and divisions of labor than the head-complement families. In the multivariate analyses, gender-role attitudes and the actual division of labor in traditionally feminine activities differentiated egalitarian and junior-partner families from those in which the wife was not employed. That is, marriage patterns in which both spouses were employed outside the home, a characteristic shared by equal-partner and junior-partner families, rather than those in which the couple shared equal financial responsibility for the household were more similar.

Involvement in masculine tasks differentiated between the patterns, especially among older couples. Both older husbands and wives who were equal partners were less engaged in masculine tasks around the home than were age peers who were in the most traditional pattern. Along with household involvement and attitudes toward gender roles, income distinguished among the marriage types with traditional families having lower incomes.

Although disagreement between spouses was significantly related to the marriage types in the one-way analyses of variance, it was not an important discriminating dimension in the multivariate assessment. Disagreement may have been indirectly linked with the patterns through

Table 6.1

Types of Contemporary Marriages

	Standardized Discriminant Function Coefficients			
	Young		Middle-Aged and Older	
	Husbands N = 168	Wives N = 168	Husbands N = 95	Wives N = 95[a]
Personal characteristics				
Education	.18	.11	-.45	.22
Income	.03	.16	.69	-.73
Household involvement				
Masculine	.18	.41	-.48	.58
Feminine	.59	.45	-.31	.56
Interpersonal and psychological characteristics				
Disagreement	-.23	-.31	.15	.02
Satisfaction	.04	-.13	-.02	-.13
Depressive symptoms	.19	.32	.15	.18
Self-concept	.13	-.21	-.09	.23
Gender-role attitudes	-.68	-.76	.68	-.31
Chi-square	63.26 $p < .001$	54.01 $p < .001$	43.53 $p < .001$	35.51 $p < .01$
Canonical correlation	.58	.56	.67	.61

[a] The number of respondents does not include the retired.

its association with the division of labor. For many of the couples, however, disagreement was correlated with the division of labor in such a way that greater sharing tended to be accompanied by somewhat more disharmony. Families in which wives assumed responsibility for traditional feminine tasks of cooking and housekeeping had fewer disagreements.

Although Quinn and Davidson (1986) suggested that decision making likely would vary by the marriage patterns, they did not find any relationship. In an unpublished analysis, we observed which partner, the husband or wife, usually made the final decision in five areas: food items to purchase, amount to spend on food and savings and investments, whether the wife should work outside the home, make and model of car to purchase, and the kind of discipline to use with children. Using a summary score across the five areas, no relationship between the nature of decision making in the families and the marriage types was found. Thus, the marriage types investigated in our research and that of others were not characterized by variant patterns of decision making.

Neither positive nor negative implications for psychological well-being of life in an equal-partner pattern versus a junior-partner pattern or a head-complement pattern were evident. For these couples, the joys that they derived from work-family roles and whether they felt good about themselves or were distressed with their lives were factors independent of the kind of marriages they maintained.

Our research and that of Scanzoni seemed to suggest that for most families, the typology of contemporary marriages is very much one of gender roles, both in terms of what spouses think of their roles and how they act them out in the household. Scanzoni (1980:127) posited that in the equal-partner arrangement, "The rights and responsibilities of each spouse relative to the occupational system, and also to the household, become relatively interchangeable." We found, however, in the multivariate analyses that equal-partner and junior-partner relationships were more similar to one another than they were to the most traditional type of marriages, irrespective of family life stage. Families in which the wives were employed tended to be distinguished from those in which they were not working outside the home by the division of household labor, especially feminine tasks, and attitudes toward gender roles.

The thinking and circumstances that likely prompted female employment and the view that it was equivalent to that of the male in the family likely also encouraged and fostered other aspects of nontraditional attitudes toward gender roles. Educational level of women may have been a driving force behind the nontraditional attitudes toward gender roles that characterized those in the most egalitarian pattern. For both younger and older women in equal-partner relationships, level of education was linked positively to nontraditional gender role attitudes ($r = .53$ and .58, $p < .01$, respectively). In contrast, among younger women who were full-time homemakers, level of education had no bearing on their attitudes toward gender roles ($r = .03$); and although the correlation between education and views of gender roles held by older women who were homemakers was stronger ($r = .20$), it was not significant.

In younger equal-partner families, educational level had a similar effect on the attitudes of husbands as well ($r = .53$, $p < .01$), whereas the thinking of their older male counterparts in egalitarian households was less closely associated with amount of education ($r = .20$, NS). Although educational level did not directly differentiate between the marriage types, in all likelihood it influenced the ideology that supported an equal-partner relationship initially. Thus, the salience of the ideological underpinnings of the marital relationship warrants further consideration. We investigate the attitudinal context of the spousal relationship through the use of a second typology, that of marital sex-role congruence. This approach draws attention to the importance and the implications of ideological similarities and differences between partners.

A MODEL OF MARITAL SEX-ROLE CONGRUENCE

The sex-role congruency model is based on the assumption that similarity in attitudinal orientations will promote the well-being of spouses. Presumably spouses with similar views will be more satisfied, may like one another more, experience less marital strain, and generally enjoy greater marital quality (Bowen & Orthner, 1983). (To be consistent with the literature on this topic, we use the term "marital sex-role congruency or congruence" rather than gender role.) In contrast to the types of marriages proposed by Scanzoni, this typology is based on gender-role attitudes rather than on the division of labor between spouses or the relative contribution of the employment of either to the family.

One view is that spouses who have arrived at a consensus on gender roles and agree on the basic rules of their relationship will maintain a marital partnership of higher quality whether both are traditional or modern. Whereas the traditional or nontraditional nature of the family structure was critical in differentiating contemporary marriage types as defined by Scanzoni, the premise of the typology of marital sex-role congruence is that traditional or modern attitudes figure less importantly in the outcomes of a marital relationship than does the agreement of spouses about appropriate behavior in their partnership. Spouses who reflect a congruent pattern should evaluate their relationship most positively and perhaps view themselves and their partner more appreciatively.

Bowen and Orthner (1983) found partial support for the hypothesis that congruence would be linked with positive marital outcomes. They observed that marriages in which the husband was traditional and the wife was modern had lower marital quality than congruent marriages (i.e., both partners modern or both traditional). Families with an egalitarian husband and a traditional wife did not differ in adjustment from the homogeneous spouses. The thinking is that an egalitarian husband may be accommodating because he is willing to forego some of his power whereas the traditional wife may be accommodating since she may lack interest in changing the existing power structure (Li & Caldwell, 1987). This pattern of incongruence may cause little distress for either spouse. Despite believing that their wives should have an opportunity to pursue independent goals, husbands may find it comforting that they are willing to give priority to family matters, and wives may benefit from knowing that they have other options should their interests change.

Li and Caldwell (1987) modified and extended the model of sex-role congruence by testing the hypothesis that both the direction of the incongruence between spouses and the magnitude of the difference in their views of gender roles would affect marital adjustment. They suggest that it is unlikely that the presence of congruence alone would result in positive adjustment or that incongruence by itself would lead to poorer adjustment. Corroborating the findings of Bowen and Orthner (1983), Li and Caldwell found that the incongruent pattern in which the wife was more egalitarian than the husband was accompanied by diminished marital adjustment, thus supporting the hypothesis that the direction of incongruence would affect marital relationships. The expectation that the magnitude of the difference between spouses' views would be a factor in adjustment was confirmed. For example, the greater the incongruence in the direction of the husband's being more egalitarian than the wife, the more positive the marital adjustment, whereas incongruence in the direction of the wife's being nontraditional and the husband traditional was accompanied by poorer adjustment.

We address several questions about correlates of patterns of sex role congruence. Were the patterns differentiated by social-status characteristics of the family (i.e., education, income, employment status of the spouses)? Were congruent or incongruent preferences for marital roles differentiated by actual involvement in masculine and feminine activities by either spouse? Were congruent or incongruent patterns associated with dynamics in the family such as disagreement over tasks, satisfaction obtained from work-family activities, or psychological well-being as reflected in self-concept or depressive symptoms? And finally, was there variation in factors linked with marital sex-role congruence or incongruence by family life stages?

Development of the Typology of Marital Sex-Role Congruence

To derive the typology of sex-role congruence, the attitudes of spouses were assessed individually, but the types were based on the views of both partners. To identify patterns of marital gender-role congruence, husbands and wives indicated who should have responsibility for four activities: earning the family income, cooking, housekeeping (except cooking and child care), and caring for and training children. Responses, noting who should have responsibility for the four work-family activities and assigned codes, ranged from "Husband always" (1) to "Wife always" (5). "Earning family income" was recoded so that the response "Husband always" was coded a "5." The scores were summed across the four questions. Thus, a higher score indicated more traditional attitudes toward work-family roles.

To obtain four patterns of marital roles subscribed to by couples, husbands and wives were categorized as having traditional or modern expectations regarding work-family tasks depending on whether their scores were above or below the means for their respective age and sex categories. Spouses with scores above or below the means for their age

Table 6.2
Patterns of Marital Role Congruence by Life Stages

Marital Role Pattern	Young Couples N = 173	Middle-Aged and Older Couples N = 163
Husband and wife nontraditional	48%	32%
Husband nontraditional and wife traditional	12%	11%
Husband traditional and wife nontraditional	17%	30%
Husband and wife traditional	24%	28%

and sex categories were described as being traditional or modern, respectively. Scores of husbands and wives were matched and cross-classified resulting in four patterns.

In one pattern, both husband and wife held nontraditional but congruent beliefs about appropriate sex roles (Modern-Modern). In a second pattern, both partners espoused more traditional, yet congruent views (Traditional-Traditional). In the two remaining types, spouses held incongruent perceptions of appropriate gender roles (Husband traditional-Wife modern and Husband modern-Wife traditional). For the analyses, the two youngest groups of couples and the two oldest groups were combined.

Marital Sex-Role Congruence and Life Stage

Patterns of marital sex role congruence differed somewhat by life stage of the couples (Table 6.2). Almost one-half of the younger partners were in the congruent pattern in which both spouses held modern perspectives. In contrast, middle-aged and older families were as likely to be in an incongruent pattern (for example, with the husband holding traditional views while the wife endorsed modern expectations) as to espouse modern attitudes together. Regardless of life stage, the least-typical pattern was for these wives to express more traditional perspectives when those of their husbands were modern; this finding is not surprising and corroborates research noted in chapter 1 suggesting that women more than men espouse nontraditional attitudes toward gender roles. Life stage figured more prominently in the gender-role attitudes of these men than in those of women, with younger men being more modern (60 percent) than middle-aged and older men (43 percent). There was less difference in the modernity of gender-role attitudes espoused by older and younger women, of whom 62 and 66 percent, respectively, were modern.

Multivariate Analyses of Marital Sex-Role Congruence

One of our interests was to determine characteristics of families in which husbands and wives held congruent or incongruent views of appropriate marital roles. That is, did comparable conditions differentiate families in which husbands and wives maintained similar or different beliefs about their roles in the family? Were benefits greater for partners in some patterns than in others, for example, were particular patterns of marital role congruence linked with greater psychological well-being? And did similar dimensions differentiate the types of families across the life stages? Were some patterns more advantageous for younger than for older couples?

To determine the extent to which social-status characteristics (education, income), employment status, assessment of responses to work-family life and psychological well-being (e.g., disagreement, satisfaction with work-family activities, self-concept), and participation in masculine and feminine activities in the household differentiated the patterns, separate discriminant analyses were conducted for men and women in the two life-stage groups (Table 6.3).

There was a significant function for each life-stage and sex group. Regardless of their life stage, the data indicated that families in which both spouses held modern views of gender roles were differentiated from the congruent-traditional pattern by some of the dimensions considered (i.e., social status, household involvement, or psychological well-being). Thus, the two congruent polar types of marriages (traditional-traditional and modern-modern) were differentiated for each of the life stages and for men and women.

Beyond the differentiation of the polar types, there were further nuances that distinguished among the mixed patterns of incongruent ideologies by sex and by life stage. In the discriminant analyses for men, regardless of age, and among younger women, individuals with similar preferences in the congruent and mixed types were grouped together and were not differentiated, irrespective of the values of the spouse. For example, among men and younger women the types of marriages in which they were modern were not distinguished from one another whether the attitudes of the partners were similar or different, that is, modern husbands with modern wives were not differentiated from modern husbands with traditional wives. But both were distinguished from traditional-traditional spouses or traditional husbands-modern wives. The polar patterns, however, were the most disparate on significant indicators such as involvement in feminine tasks for men and younger women. Among older women, congruent modern spouses were differentiated from all of the other patterns.

What factors distinguished among the patterns of marital role con-

Relationships and Well-Being Over The Life Stages

Table 6.3
Marital Role Congruence

| | Standardized Discriminant Function Coefficients | | | |
| | Young N = 173 | | Middle-Aged and Older N = 163 | |
	Husbands	Wives	Husbands	Wives
Personal characteristics				
Education	-.27	.15		
Income	-.16	.38	.38	-.26
Employment, wife	.52	-.47	.34	.17
Employment, husband			.33	-.11
Household involvement				
Masculine	-.22	.34	-.21	.18
Feminine	.64	-.52	.68	.84
Interpersonal and psychological well-being				
Disagreement	-.14	.15	-.07	.06
Satisfaction	.31	-.03	.30	-.10
Depressive symptoms				
Self-concept	.15	.20	-.22	.11
Chi-square	80.73 p <.01	84.95 p <.01	54.33 p <.01	60.13 p <.01
Canonical correlation	.63	.61	.45	.55

gruence? For younger partners, wives' employment and involvement of both sexes in feminine household activities most consistently distinguished among the patterns. Women in families in which both spouses held modern views were much more likely to be employed regardless of life stage, although in the discriminant analysis female employment differentiated among the patterns only for younger partners. For example, 70 percent of wives in younger families in which both spouses held congruent-modern views were employed compared to only 15 percent of the women in relationships with congruent-traditional perceptions of marital roles. To the degree that female employment was an indicator of somewhat nontraditional behavior in these families, these spouses acted on their beliefs, so that there was a close link between what they thought should be and what they were able to attain in their work-family lives. As we shall see, however, among older families the strength of congruent nontraditional expectations of spouses was not sufficient to be associated with less-conventional participation in feminine tasks by employed wives.

Female employment and participation in feminine activities jointly distinguished between the congruent-modern pattern and all other patterns among the younger couples in the following way. In families with nontraditional spouses, employed wives were less involved in feminine tasks and their husbands were more active. This finding was not observed for the other patterns of marital role congruence. In contrast, among older families in the congruent-traditional pattern, wives' employment did not occasion less participation by women in feminine activities. Older traditional employed women were even more involved than homemakers in feminine tasks, perhaps indicating an effort to compensate for their less-traditional work behavior and bring it into line with their less-modern values.

Involvement in feminine tasks was the most important factor that discriminated among the marital patterns of older men and women. Older women in modern congruent marriages were significantly less involved in feminine housework than their age peers in the other three types of relationships ($F = 20.12$, $p < .001$). When older men held traditional values, regardless of the views of their spouses, they were less involved in the household ($F = 21.28$, $p < .001$). Therefore, modern wives with traditional husbands received less help around the house than wives with more modern husbands.

One-way analyses of variance indicated that disagreement between spouses about work-family activities was more frequent in the congruent-modern pattern than in the congruent-traditional group for both younger ($F = 3.15$, $p < .05$) and older men ($F = 2.90$, $p < .05$), and younger women ($F = 20.12$, $p < .001$). Contrary to some earlier findings about diminished marital adjustment in the pattern in which the husband is traditional and the wife modern, we observed the most conflict among couples who shared modern attitudes. In fact, younger traditional men with modern wives, a combination earlier identified as perhaps being problematic, reported less disagreement than was found in congruent marriages in which both spouses were modern. In the multivariate analyses, however, disagreement was not very salient in differentiating the marital role patterns.

Our findings provide some evidence on the question of whether well-being is fostered more in one family pattern than in another. Satisfaction with work-family roles and regard for oneself did not thrive in congruent patterns any more than in those with less agreement between partners. Finally, for these men and women incongruent patterns were not any more distressing than more harmonious marriages as reflected in depressive symptoms. Although congruence influenced some aspects of the spousal relationship, living with a spouse who held somewhat different expectations from one's own usually was not especially stressful for these couples. Rather, the most direct link between family and personal characteristics and the patterns was reflected in actual behavior (e.g., female employment or household involvement) instead of in observations on interpersonal relationships in the family or personal well-being.

Like that recounted in the previous chapter, evidence again was provided that highlights the importance of gender-role attitudes and actual behavior in the household in describing the kind of marital patterns that families may evolve. Although these younger men were especially more modern than their middle-aged and older peers in both their beliefs and subsequent behavior, attitudes toward gender roles seemed to have shaped the structure of some family activities in a powerful way regardless of life stage.

Analyses of the typology of marital role congruence underscored the importance of agreement of both spouses on nontraditional beliefs if the most egalitarian division of labor in feminine tasks were to be maintained. If either spouse held traditional beliefs, then behavior in the family tended to be less modern. Evidently to sustain a nontraditional life-style may be more difficult than to maintain a traditional one, and the degree of ease in doing so is enhanced by the reciprocal support of the values of both spouses. Families with congruent patterns, whether traditional or modern, were somewhat more likely to realize their preferences for gender roles.

SUMMARY AND DISCUSSION

In this chapter two typologies of marriages—types of contemporary marriages and patterns of sex-role congruence—were considered. Both typologies of marital patterns included polar types of traditional versus more modern marriages. Clearly, female employment, work in the household, and views of gender roles were central in differentiating the ways in which spouses structured their lives. One typology focused on agreement between spouses on attitudes toward gender roles, whereas in the other female employment was a critical dimension. Modern attitudes toward marital roles, congruent thinking between spouses about these roles, and employment of women were linked.

The support for the most modern behavior was drawn from reciprocal values held by spouses with nontraditional perspectives on gender roles accompanying shared employment, joint financial responsibility for the household, and more modern behavior within the family. As reflected in the typology of marriages proposed by Scanzoni (1980), a critical factor that differentiated one pattern from another was whether wives were employed rather than whether they assumed equal responsibility for providing financially for the family. To the degree that the personal and family characteristics we considered were important, they differentiated the egalitarian and junior-partner families from those in which the wife was a homemaker. Our research partially supported that of Scanzoni because equal partners, both men and women across age groups, preferred both interchangeability in roles outside the household, as reflected in the employment of the wife, and interchangeability in the domestic arena as well.

But what were the consequences of life in a traditional versus a more modern marriage or in one in which views of partners were articulated similarly in contrast to those in which they defined their activities differently? Initially we asked several questions about the social context in which these patterns existed and their linkage to the well-being of spouses. Social-status characteristics did not directly differentiate between patterns in either typology. Rather, education, for example, may have had significance for socialization and eventually was reflected in gender-role ideology in adulthood.

In the analyses of marital role congruence, for the two life stages considered and for both husbands and wives the polar patterns (i.e., modern-modern, traditional-traditional) were distinguished from one another. This indicated the strength of congruence in influencing activities both within and outside the household, that is, involvement in feminine tasks and in female employment. Masculine household activities were independent of marital role congruence.

Although in both typologies, disagreement between spouses seemed to be more prevalent in nontraditional marriages, conflict between partners was related to the patterns through its relationship to less-conventional views of gender roles and practicing them in the family. Bowen and Orthner (1983) found that marriages with a traditional husband and a modern wife had the lowest marital quality. One aspect of their measure of marital quality was disagreement. We did not find that disagreement was highest among traditional husbands married to non-traditional wives. Our research, however, included spouses from a wider range of ages and a greater variety of occupational backgrounds than the military couples studied by Bowen and Orthner.

In general the type of marriage was not associated with psychological well-being. Although Scanzoni suggested that future research might consider variation in self-esteem across the types of marriages and speculated that positive self-regard would be higher among junior partners, we did not find evidence to confirm this thinking. A strength of our research was the inclusion of husbands whereas some earlier work had studied only wives.

Our research suggested that both the employment configuration of spouses and the congruency of their views of gender roles differentiated marriages on dimensions that would ensure that some aspects of life in them likely would be quite different. But employing either typology, we did not find that any one style of marriage was clearly more distressing or fulfilling than another. Similarly, congruence on gender-role perspectives was not especially a source of comfort.

7

The Self-Concept in an Intimate Relationship

One of the most important factors in the study of human behavior is the self-concept. How individuals define themselves has profound implications for their behavior in a variety of social situations. Past research has demonstrated diverse social behavior associated with a positive or negative self-concept. It has been found that a high self-concept is associated with success and positive interpersonal skills. Individuals with a positive self-concept are socially at ease, popular, confident of their opinions and judgments, and assertive in social relationships. Individuals with a negative self-concept suggest an unhappy contrast. They tend to be socially anxious and ineffective. They view interpersonal relationships as threatening, lack confidence in their own activities, and are easily hurt by criticism by others.

The consequences of a negative self-concept have particular significance for dysfunctional individual behavior. A low self-concept has been implicated as a contributory factor in depression (Ingham, Kreitman, Miller, Sashidharan & Surtees, 1986), anxiety (Luck & Heiss, 1972), child abuse (Shorkey, 1980), helplessness (Storr, 1979), and alcohol and drug abuse (Brehm & Black, 1968).

In the study of intimate relationships the level of the self-concept has been found to have a significant impact on conditions of the relationship. A positive self-concept is linked with a willingness to self-disclose (Pederson & Breglio, 1968), to be less defensive (Berger, 1973), to be interpersonally receptive (Libby & Yaklevich, 1973), and less likely to engage in a destructive approach to problem solving (Rusbult, Morrow & Johnson, 1987). A lower self-concept is linked with greater dependency (Friedman, 1976) and jealousy (White, 1981). The critical role of the self in examining human behavior suggests its importance in the study of marital role relationship and well-being over the life course. Successful family functioning to a large degree depends on partners having the social resources that are the consequence of a feeling of self-worth. Since marriage is a social arrangement that brings two people together in many intimate aspects of life, all of one's personality, including the self, affects success or failure in this arrangement. Because of the duration and intensity of the interaction that takes place within a marriage, the marital relationship provides a good example of interacting personalities, in which the self could have serious implications. In developing a framework for examining marriage and family relationships, Mangus (1957:203) has noted the importance of the self-concept: "It seems safe to say that one of the most useful constructs that has been developed for the understanding of personality and behavior is the concept of the social-self. . . . The social-self becomes the chief instrument by which a person's conduct is ordered and directed toward motive satisfaction."

However, the impact of the self on the marital relationship has received relatively modest attention. Earlier research has demonstrated a positive relationship between the self and marital quality (Barnett & Nietzel, 1979; Sharpley & Kahn, 1980) and role performance (Schafer & Braito, 1979). These investigations generally concluded that the self can be considered as a valuable skill or resource contributing to the marital relationship. A positive self-concept is seen as making the marriage partner more interesting, competent, or accepting or as having other positive qualities to contribute to marriage quality.

The typical approach in examining the self is to focus on the self-concept as a singular entity correlated with a variety of individual or interpersonal behaviors. The analysis in this chapter, however, will not be limited to a singular conception of the self. Rather, a more comprehensive approach in examining the role of self in well-being in relationships across the family life cycle is the symbolic-interactionist construct of the *reflected self* (Cooley, 1902; Mead, 1934). This approach defines the self as a product of interaction with others. The self-concept is learned from the reactions of others through role taking in which one interprets the responses of others toward oneself and thereby defines a self-concept. The actor therefore comes to see herself as she perceives that others see her. This reflected or "looking-glass" notion of the self necessarily assumes a social self in which there are perceptual and evaluative components lodged in interaction that define the self-concept. There are three components that constitute a reflected self-concept: (1) how the individual evaluates himself or herself, (2) how the individual believes others evaluate him or her, and (3) how others actually evaluate the individual (Rosenberg, 1981). Thus, the self-concept is determined by others' actual appraisal and the individual's subjective perception of others' appraisal.

The major assumption of this interactionist model of the self is the process of role taking, through which persons regard themselves from the point of view of others. This process of reflected appraisals is the cornerstone of the symbolic interactionist perspective on self-concept formation (Rosenberg, 1979). The actual appraisals and behavior of significant others do not necessarily have a direct effect on a person's self-concept. Rather, others' appraisals are reflected through a person's perceptions; that becomes the reality on which a person organizes, changes, or validates a self-concept.

From the interactionist perspective it is clear that to understand the self more fully it is essential to understand the components that underlie the self. Furthermore, to understand the relationship of the self to well-being it is useful to investigate the influence of these components on that relationship. It is not the self-concept as product that has sole influence on well-being and marital quality. Equally important are how marriage partners perceive that their spouses evaluate them and how their spouses actually evaluate them.

How marriage partners perceive that their spouses feel about them may be reflected in how they approach and perform their various marital roles, the nature of interaction with the spouses, and their evaluation of their marital relationships. If marriage partners perceive that their spouses hold them in low esteem, they are less likely to be effective in marital interaction or to feel good about their own performances (Schafer & Braito, 1979). On the other hand, if marriage partners actually hold negative assessments of their spouses, they are less likely to expect much or to be satisfied with their spouses' contributions to marital interaction. Such attitudes are communicated to the spouses and may affect the spouses' appraisal of the quality of the marital relationship.

To study the impact of the reflected self on the marriage relationship, four analyses will be conducted: (1) a comparison of self-concept at different family life stages, (2) specification of a causal model of the reflected self, (3) the effect of the reflected self on psychological well-being, and (4) the effect of the reflected self on marital quality.

ASSESSING THE SELF-CONCEPT

A global self-concept measure was used to examine the three elements of the reflected self-concept. The marriage partners' self-concepts, their appraisals of their spouses, and their perceptions of their spouses' appraisals of them, were measured through the use of a set of self-descriptive adjectives [arranged in the order of the semantic differential].

Table 7.1
Reflected Self-Concept across Family Life Stages

	Stage 1		Stage 2		Stage 3		Stage 4	
	Husband N = 85	Wife	Husband N = 88	Wife	Husband N = 81	Wife	Husband N = 82	Wife
Self-concept	5.92	5.82	5.87	5.66	5.78	5.70	5.74	5.72
Perceived self-concept	5.90	5.79	5.94	5.69	5.89	5.91	5.98	5.92
Social self-concept	6.01	6.17	6.16	6.16	6.01	6.17	6.17	6.24

Scores are based on a seven-point scale, with 7 representing a positive self-concept and 1 representing a negative self-concept; mean socres are given.

The form of the question and the items included were drawn from Sherwood's (1962) self-concept inventory. As a result of a pretest, seven adjectives were selected for inclusion in the self-concept scale (likable/not likable, capable/incapable, self-confident/not self-confident, satisfied/frustrated, useful/useless, intelligent/unintelligent, friendly/unfriendly). A seven-point response scale was used for each item. Respondents were presented with the seven items and asked (1) to describe themselves, using seven adjective pairs; (2) to describe their spouse, using the same adjective pairs; and (3) to indicate how they thought their spouse would describe them, using the same adjective pairs. Scores were computed for each of the three measures by summing the respondents' ratings for the seven items. The data were coded so that a higher score represented a more positive appraisal. The alpha reliability coefficients for each of the three measures were as follows: self-concept, .78; appraisal of spouse, .78; and perceived appraisal by spouse, .82. These three components of the self will be defined using Rosenberg's (1981) terminology: Self-Concept (SC); Perception of Spouse's Evaluation = Perceived Self-Concept (PSC); and Spousal Actual Evaluation = Social Self-Concept (SSC).

Self-Concept across Life Stages

The mean scores for self-concept, perceived self-concept, and social self-concept for partners at different life stages are presented in Table 7.1. There appears to be only a slight and insignificant decline of the self-concept at different marital life stages for both partners, with the greatest decline coming for women between Stage 1 and Stage 2. Therefore, across the family life stages the self-concept of marital partners appears to be relatively stable. There was not an appreciable decline in self-concept occurring under conditions in which there may be a questioning of self-worth, such as in the cases of empty-nest families or elderly families. For married couples there was only a slight tendency for husbands to have a more positive self-concept than for their wives. But the difference was significant only for couples at Stage 2 ($t = 2.03$, $p < .05$).

The assessment of the self-concept over the family life stages suggests a rather stable construction that does not necessarily increase or decrease because of major role transitions that define life stages. A more dramatic difference is found between partners' evaluation of themselves and their evaluation of their spouse. There was a significant tendency for both husbands and wives to evaluate their partner (SSC) more positively than they evaluated themselves (SC). Such differential assessments were due to the type of evaluations being made. These are established relationships and, by definition, successful relationships. Thus, there is the tendency to place a positive evaluation on a spouse. The lower assessment of self may be due to the subjects' intimate awareness of their own faults, shortcomings, and failures as they make a subjective assessment of self.

THE REFLECTED SELF-CONCEPT WITHIN THE MARRIAGE RELATIONSHIP

The first section examined the marital partners' reflected self-concept over the family life stages. This section will articulate a general causal model of the reflected self that can be used in the study of well-being. The key element in this model is the role-taking process of the perceived self-concept.

The importance of role taking to the self-concept has been restated and theoretically articulated by Kinch (1963). He defined a causal chain in which the actual responses of others have a direct effect on a person's perception of others' responses, which in turn affect the self-concept. The influence of the actual responses of others on the self-concept is defined as a derived proposition and not as having a direct causal link to the self.

The correlation coefficients between self-concept and perceptions of spouses' evaluations (perceived self-concept = PSC) for both husbands ($.701$, $p < .001$) and wives ($.767$, $p < .001$) were significant in a positive direction: the more positively partners felt their spouses evaluated them, the more positively they evaluated themselves.

The correlation coefficients between marriage partners' self-concepts and the actual appraisal by the spouses (social self-concept = SSC) were also significant in a positive direction for both marriage partners. The more highly partners evaluated themselves, the more highly their spouses also evaluated them (.38, $p < .001$, and .29, $p < .001$, for husbands and wives, respectively). These relationships, though significant, are less strong than the correlations between self-concept and perceived evaluation of spouse. In other words, the perception of the spouse's evaluation is more closely related to self-concept than is the spouse's actual evaluation.

A third set of correlations addresses the issue of the accuracy of perceiving others' opinions. The correlation coefficients between partners' perceptions of spouses' evaluations of them (PSC) and spouses' actual evaluations (SSC) are .39 ($p < .001$) for husbands' perceptions and wives' actual appraisals and .46 ($p < .001$) for wives' perceptions and husbands' actual appraisals. This finding suggests that there is agreement between how partners think their spouses evaluate them and how their spouses actually evaluate them. The subjects are demonstrating moderate role-taking accuracy in their perceptions of their spouses' appraisals of them.

The next step in the analysis is to place the three components of the reflected self into a simple linear-recursive model via path analysis. Path analysis is a statistical technique that specifies the theoretically causal relationship among variables. It has become recognized as valuable in quantifying and interpreting causal theory in sociology and social psychology. It is selected for the current analysis because it allows a specification of the causal structure in the interactionist model of the self-concept. Use of this statistical approach provides a method of *decomposing*, or specifying the total effects of independent variables into their direct and indirect effects.

The approach used in this analysis is that of Alwin and Hauser (1975), who specified a distinction between associations and effects and provided a method for analyzing the decomposition of total effects of independent variables into their direct and indirect effects. The zero-order correlation approach demonstrates the total association between the variables that make up the self. The total effect of one variable on another is that effect which is not due to the variables' common causes or correlations among their causes. The indirect effects in a linear-recursive model are those parts of a variable's total effect on the dependent variable that are mediated by an intervening variable. The direct effects then are simply that portion of the total effect of one variable on another that are not mediated by an intervening variable. Path analysis allows for the decomposition of the direct and indirect effects of significant others' actual appraisal on a person's self-concept. This analysis thereby articulates the importance of role taking as the mediating variable between others' actual appraisals and the self-concept. The decomposition of the total effects of partners' social self-concept on their partners' self-concept is presented in Table 7.2.

It is clear from the data presented in the table that when the effect of

Table 7.2

Decomposition of Total Effects of Spouses' Actual Appraisals into Direct and Indirect Effects for Husbands and Wives, (Beta) N = 336 couples

Dependent Variables	Independent Variables	Total Effect	Indirect Effect via Perception of Spouses' Appraisal	Direct Effect
Model 1 Husbands' self-concept	Wives' social self-concept	.375	.326	.049
Model 2 Wives' self-concept	Husbands' social self-concept	.292	.293	-.001

husbands' perceptions of wives' appraisals (PSC-H) and wives' perceptions of husbands' appraisals (PSC-W) were controlled, there was little direct effect of the actual appraisal of the spouse on husbands' and wives' self-concepts. Analysis of the decomposition of effects reveals that, for the first model, the total effect of wives' appraisals on husbands' self-concept is .38; but of that total effect, .33 was an indirect effect via husbands' perceptions of wives' appraisals, leaving a direct effect of only .05.

The data for the second model, the effects of husbands' appraisals on wives' self-concept, demonstrated the same results as the preceding analysis. The total effect of husbands' appraisals on wives' self-concepts was .29. This total effect was due exclusively to the indirect effect of .29 mediated by wives' perceptions of husbands' appraisals, leaving no direct effect. Clearly, in this analysis, marriage partners' appraisals of each other had an effect on their partners' self-concept, but that effect was indirect and was mediated through the process of role taking.

These findings conform to the basic model of the reflected self by highlighting the importance of the role-taking process through which the appraisals of significant others become factors in shaping the concept. It is this role-taking process that has implications for the well-being and the perceived marital quality of marriage partners.

EFFECT OF THE SELF-CONCEPT ON PSYCHOLOGICAL WELL-BEING

Now that a model of the reflected self has been developed and tested, we will use it to examine the effect of the self-concept on psychological well-being and marital quality. The general model that will be followed

Figure 7.1
Relationship between Reflected Self-Concept and Psychological Well-Being and Marital Quality

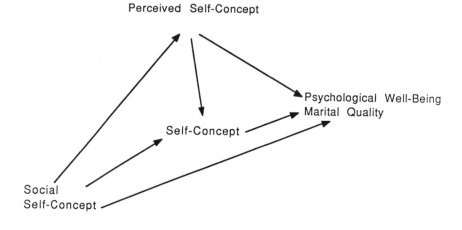

Perceived Self-Concept

Psychological Well-Being
Marital Quality

Self-Concept

Social
Self-Concept

in this analysis is presented in Figure 7.1. Again, this analysis will not rely solely on the self-concept as a singular construct but rather also will specify the direct and indirect effects of spouses' actual and perceived evaluation on well-being. Consequently a more complete assessment of the relationship between the self-concept and well-being can be evaluated. As examined in earlier chapters, our indicator of level of psychological well-being will be depressive symptoms.

In the study of the relationship between self and depressive symptoms, it has been demonstrated that a negative self-concept contributes to feelings of depression (Ingham et al., 1986; Luck & Heiss, 1972). To explain this correspondence Beck (1974) specified a self-concept model in the explanation of depression. He stated that the basis for depression is a negative cognitive set. The depressed person has a negative view of himself or herself as well as of the world and the future. The depressed state is secondary and the product of negative self-cognitions. Abramson, Seligman, and Teasdale (1978) take a somewhat similar position in specifying depression as consisting of major disturbances in a person's self-view.

To explicate more completely the effect of the self on depressive symptoms, we will use the recursive-path model demonstrated in the previous section with depressive symptoms as the dependent variable. The causal pattern predicted in the model is that the self-concept will have a sig-

Table 7.3

Decomposition of Effects of the Reflected Self-Concept on Husbands' and Wives' Depressive Symptoms, (Beta) N = 336 couples

Dependent Variables	Independent Variables	Total Effect	Indirect Effects Via PSC	SC	Direct Effect
Husbands' depressive symptoms	SSC, Wife	-.28	-.14	-.01	-.13
	PSC, Husband	-.31		-.18	-.13
	SC, Husband	-.25			-.25
Wives' depressive symptoms	SSC, Husband	-.11	-.15	.00	.04
	PSC, Wife	-.37		-.14	-.23
	SC, Wife	-.19			-.19

SC = self-concept
PSC = perceived self-concept
SSC = social self-concept

nificant direct effect on depressive symptoms and that the perceived self-concept (PSC) and the social self-concept (SSC) have both direct and indirect effects on depressive symptoms. Stated otherwise, how people think their spouses evaluate them and how their spouses actually do evaluate them will have an influence on their feelings of depression.

The decomposition of effects of the reflected self on subjects' depressive symptoms are presented in Table 7.3. The analysis in this table does not include reflected-self variables as dependent variables, as that analysis was conducted in the previous section. Only depressive symptoms will be considered as a dependent variable. Two forms of the model were analyzed, one each for husbands and wives. For husbands, the total effect of self-concept ($-.25$, $p < .001$), perceived self-concept ($-.31$, $p < .001$), and social self-concept ($-.28$, $p < .001$) were significantly related to depressive symptoms. The lower these components of the self, the greater the depressive symptoms.

What is particularly interesting in this analysis, however, is the importance of the role-taking process represented by perceived self-concept. For the husbands, 51 percent ($-.14$) of the total effect of wives' actual appraisal (SSC) of their husbands on husbands' feelings of depression was mediated through the husbands' PSC. In other words, how the husbands thought their wives evaluated them had an influence on the relationship between wives' actual appraisal of husbands and husbands' feelings of depression. Further, of that total effect of husbands' PSC on husbands' depression ($.-31$), 42 percent was direct and 58 percent was mediated through the husbands' self-concept. Thus, almost one-half of the effect of husbands' perceptions of their wives' evaluation of them was direct and not transferred through the husbands' self-concept. Therefore, the model demonstrated that, for husbands, depression was the consequence of all three components of the self, with the husbands' perceived self-concept having both a direct and mediating effect.

For wives a similar pattern was observed with two exceptions. Whereas both self-concept ($-.19$, $p < .01$) and perceived self-concept ($-.37$, $p < .001$) were significantly related to wives' depression, the total effect of husbands' evaluation of their wives on wives' depressive symptoms was not significant ($-.11$, $p < .05$) and considerably smaller than the same relationship for husbands. But, as with husbands, much of the effect of the husbands' appraisal of wives on their depression was expressed through the wives' self-concept.

Another difference between husbands and wives appears to be the importance of the perceived self-concept. The data seem to indicate that perceived self-concept was more important for wives' feelings of depression than it was for their husbands'. The total effect of PSC on depression was only slightly larger for wives than for husbands ($-.37$ versus $-.31$). However, for wives, 62 percent of that effect was direct and not mediated through the self-concept, whereas for husbands only 42 percent of the total effect of PEC was a direct effect on depression. The data suggest that wives placed more importance on how they think their spouses feel about them than did husbands, and their perception of a negative assessment had a more direct relationship on feelings of depression.

Conclusions About the Self and Depression

For both husbands and wives it was the role playing or imagery process represented by the perceived self-concept that was of particular interest in this analysis. Spouses' perception of how their partner evaluated them had clear implications for their psychological well-being. If partners assume their spouses have a low assessment of them, this will lead to a diminished sense of self-worth. As Abramson et al. (1978) suggest, this disturbance of the self view has consequences for experiencing depression. Therefore, it is important to note that, in understanding depression as a consequence of low self-assessment, a complete picture cannot be arrived at without taking into account the factors that underlie the self. Whereas low self-concept has been found here and elsewhere to be a contributory factor to depression, of equal importance are the actual and perceived appraisals of significant others. These two components are important in explaining depression because first and foremost they define the self-concept. But they also have a direct influence on depression independent of the self-concept. If individuals perceive that their spouses have a negative perception of them, they will as self-theory predicts have a more negative self-concept. Also, as this analysis demonstrates, if marriage partners felt that their spouses did not have a high evaluation of them, they were likely to feel discouraged and to demonstrate symptoms of depression; if the spouses actually had a negative evaluation, this was likely communicated through interaction in the relationship and contributed to partners' feelings of depression.

THE SELF-CONCEPT AND MARITAL QUALITY

The model of the reflected self that was used to explicate the relationship between the self and psychological well-being will also be used to examine the influence of the self on marital quality. It is likely that not only the self-concept will have implications for marital quality but so also will the reflected components of the self. How marriage partners feel that their spouses evaluate them may influence how they approach and perform their various marital roles. If marriage partners perceive they are held in low esteem by their spouses, they are less likely to be effective in the marital interaction or to feel good about their own performances. If marriage partners actually hold negative assessments of their spouses, they will not expect much or be satisfied with their spouses' contributions to marital interaction.

The three indicators selected to measure marital quality were role-performance evaluations of self and spouse and marital role disagreement. The five roles selected for the analysis included the household tasks of cooking and housekeeping, the interpersonal roles of companionship to spouse and caring for children, and the provider role.

As with the analysis of psychological well-being, it was proposed that the indicators of marital quality would be dependent on the effects of the three components of the reflected self-concept. To conduct this analysis, three path models were used, one each for the three measures of marital quality. Each of the three models was tested for husbands and wives separately, resulting in six separate path analyses. The decomposition of the total effects into the direct and indirect effects are presented in Tables 7.4 through 7.6.

Model 1. The Self-Concept and Role Performance of Self

In this model we examine the influence of the components of the reflected self-concept on the respondents' evaluation of their own role performance. The direct and indirect effects of the reflected self on marital partners' evaluation of their role performance is presented in Table 7.4. Wives' actual appraisals of husbands (SSC-W) did not

Table 7.4

Decomposition of Effects of the Reflected Self-Concept on Husbands' and Wives' Evaluation of Their Own Marital Role Performances, (Beta) N = 336 couples

Dependent Variables	Independent Variables	Total Effect	Indirect Effects Via		Direct Effect
			PSC	SC	
Model 1. Husbands:					
Role performance of self	SSC, Wife	.07	.09	.01	-.03
	PSC, Husband	.18		.16	.02
	SC, Husband	.23			.23
Model 1. Wives:					
Role performance of self	SSC, Husband	.05	.13	.01	-.09
	PSC, Wife	.33		.16	.17
	SC, Wife	.20			.20

have a significant effect on husbands' own role-performance evaluations (.07). Husbands' perceptions of wives' appraisals (PSC-H) had a significant effect on their role-performance evaluations (.18, $p <$ .01), but most of that effect (89 percent) was mediated through husbands' self-concept (.16), leaving a direct effect of only .02. Husbands' self-concept had a significant direct effect on their role-performance evaluations (.23, $p < .01$). Husbands' self-concept was more important for their role-performance evaluation of themselves than either wives' actual or husbands' perception of wives' evaluation of them.

For the wives, a similar pattern was found. However, wives' perceptions of husbands' appraisals (PSC-W) had a significant effect on their role-performance evaluation (.33, $p < .001$), with 47 percent of that total effect expressed via wives' self-concepts (.16), leaving a direct effect of .17.

In examining the relationship of the reflected self-concept to role-performance evaluation, we found that perception of spouses' appraisals had an influence on the respondents' role-performance evaluations. However, much of that influence was indirect, being mediated through the self-concept. Furthermore, actual appraisals of spouses (SSC) did not have a direct or indirect influence on the marriage partners' perceptions of their own role performances. Therefore, for both husbands and wives, the self-concept was the most critical variable, both in demonstrating a significant direct influence and in mediating the effects of perceptions of spouses' evaluations on the dependent variable of role-performance evaluation of the self. How respondents felt about them-

Table 7.5
Decomposition of Effects of the Reflected Self-Concept on Husbands' and
Wives' Evaluation of Their Spouses' Role Performances, (Beta) N = 336
couples

Dependent Variables	Independent Variables	Total Effect	Indirect Effects Via PSC	SC	Direct Effect
Model 2. Husbands:					
Role performance of spouse	SSC, Wife	.13	.13	.00	.00
	PSC, Husband	.29		-.01	.30
	SC, Husband	-.02			-.02
Model 2. Wives:					
Role performance of spouse	SSC, Husband	.11	.08	.00	.03
	PSC, Wife	.19		.12	.07
	SC, Wife	.15			.15

selves was more important for their own role-performance evaluation than how their spouses evaluated them.

Model 2. The Self-Concept and Role Performance of Spouse

In Model 2, we investigated the influence of the self-concept on subjects' evaluation of their spouses' role performance. Whereas in Model 1 we found the self-concept affected respondents' assessment of their own role performance, will the self also affect an assessment of their partners' role performance? The effects demonstrated in the second model, presented in Table 7.5, were quite different from those found in the first model. Spouses' actual evaluations of their marriage partners (SSC) had a small but significant total effect on married partners' evaluations of their spouses' role performances for both husbands (.13, $p < .05$) and wives (.11, $p < .05$). However, for both partners the greater part of that total effect was mediated via the marriage partners' perceptions of their spouses' appraisals of them (PSC), leaving virtually no direct effect. For husbands, perceptions of their spouses' appraisals of them (PSC-H) had a significant total effect of .29 ($p < .001$) on their evaluations of their wives' role performances. This total effect was not mediated via husbands' self-concepts and was therefore attributable almost exclusively to a direct effect. For wives there was also a significant total effect (.19, $p < .01$) of their perceptions of husbands' appraisals (PSC-W) on their evaluations of husbands' role performances. Of this total effect, however, 61 percent was mediated via wives' self-concept, leaving a direct effect of .07.

Table 7.6
Decomposition of Effects of the Reflected Self-Concept on Husbands' and
Wives' Role Disagreement, (Beta) N = 336 couples

Dependent Variables	Independent Variables	Total Effect	Indirect Effects Via PSC	SC	Direct Effect
Model 3. Husbands: Disagreement	SSC, Wife	-.21	-.11	.00	-.10
	PSC, Husband	-.23		.07	-.30
	SC, Husband	-.09			-.09
Model 3. Wives: Disagrement	SSC, Husband	-.12	-.11	.05	-.06
	PSC, Wife	-.26		.00	-.26
	SC, Wife	-.08			-.08

The single most important variable influencing the evaluation of spouses' role performance was the perceived self-concept (how the individuals perceive that their spouses evaluate them). The more positively the subjects feel that their spouses evaluate them, the more positively the subjects evaluate their spouses' role performance. This suggests a type of reciprocity in which individuals respond favorably to others who they feel like them.

Model 3. The Self-Concept and Role Disagreement

The final indicator of marital quality is role disagreement. Can the reflected self help us further understand the occurrence of role disagreement in the marital relationship? The data presented in Table 7.6 examines the causal paths between the reflected self-concept and role disagreement. For husbands, their wives' actual appraisals of them (SSC-W) had a significant total effect on their assessments of marital role disagreement ($-.21$, $p < .001$); the higher the wives' evaluations of their husbands, the lower the husbands' perceptions of marital role disagreement. Of that total effect, 54 percent was transmitted via husbands' perceptions of their wives' evaluations of them (PSC-H), leaving a direct effect of $-.10$ unmediated by the variables in the model. For wives there was a total effect of $-.12$ ($p < .05$) of husbands' actual appraisals of their wives (SSC-H) on wives' perceptions of marital role disagreement, but 89 percent of that total effect ($-.11$) was transmitted via wives' perceptions of husbands' evaluations (PSC-W). For both husbands and wives, perception of spouses' appraisals (PSC) had a direct effect on marital role disagreement that was unmediated by the self-concept variable (for husbands, $-.30$, $p < .001$; for wives, $-.26$, $p < .001$). The more positively husbands and wives felt their spouses evaluated them, the lower their perception of marital role disagreement. However, for both husbands and wives, their own self-concept did not have a significant effect on perceived marital role disagreement.

Conclusions about Self and Marital Quality

This analysis of marital quality introduces a new look at the role of the self-concept in the marital relationship. Instead of being limited by the singular analysis of the effect of marriage partners' self-concept on the marriage relationship, this study broadened the analysis to include the perceptions that underlie the self-concept. It is not a partner's self-concept alone that influences marital quality but also the spouse's perceived and actual evaluation of his or her partner. To ignore these components of the reflected self is to overlook important dynamics of the marital relationship.

This study attempted to reassess the relationship of the self-concept to marital quality using the construct of the reflected self. When assessment of one's own role performance is taken as an indicator of marital quality, then the self-concept is an important predictive variable, as was demonstrated in Model 1. This suggests a generalization from positive self-regard to a positive assessment of one's own marital role performance. However, when the assessments of marital quality shift to an assessment of the spouse's role performance and an assessment of role disagreement, it is the perception of spouse's appraisal that becomes the important predictive variable, not the self-concept. The more positively marriage partners feel that their spouses describe them, the higher their evaluation of their spouses' role performances and the less role disagreement they perceive.

The data suggest for the couples studied that, when partners judged their own role performances, they depended in part on their own self-regard to make those evaluations. When partners judged their spouses' performances and marital role disagreement, they appeared to depend more on how they believed their spouses evaluated them. These findings are consistent with the research of Jones, Knurek, and Regan (1973) on reciprocal liking and suggest under certain conditions assessment of marital quality may be a function of reciprocity. Partners who perceive that their spouses evaluate them highly reciprocate by a positive evaluation of both their partners' contribution to the marriage relationship and their interaction with their partners. This point of view is suggested by Blau (1964), who notes that, in an intimate relationship, partners' feelings for and commitment to each other are reciprocal and must develop at roughly the same pace if feelings of exploitation or entrapment are to be avoided.

CONCLUSION

This chapter has introduced a new look at the role of the self in the study of the marital relationship. Our analysis examined two aspects of the marital relationship, psychological well-being and marital quality. Instead of examining the self as a singular concept, we introduced the model of the reflected self. It is not just how marriage partners feel about themselves that influences their psychological well-being but also how their spouses feel about them and how they believe their spouses evaluate them. It is these overlooked variables, perception of spouses' appraisal and, to a lesser extent, spouses' actual appraisal, that may account for much of the relationship found between self-concept and depressive symptoms and marital quality.

Gender-Role Attitudes, Characteristics of Employment, and Well-Being of Single and Married Employed Mothers

In this chapter, employment characteristics and gender-role attitudes are considered in relation to self-concept and depressive symptoms of single parents (n = 52) and married women (n = 87). Both groups of women were employed and had children living at home.

Despite increases in single-parent families, a pathological model labeling their life-styles as deviant and inadequate has characterized much of the literature, especially the early writing (Brandwein, Brown & Fox, 1974). From this perspective, single-parent families are viewed as broken or in some way abnormal (Gongla & Thompson, 1987). In turn, the deficits and inadequacies attributed to these families are believed to contribute to psychological distress for both parents and children.

Two aspects of life, economic and domestic, have been viewed as especially stressful for single parents. The economic situation of single-parent women whose incomes are less than one-third of those of two-parent families is well-documented (Cohen, Johnson, Lewis & Brook, 1990; Gongla & Thompson, 1987). Most single parents are women who usually undergo a marked reduction in income with the transition in marital status (Arendell, 1986). Furthermore, the difference between incomes of husband-wife households and those of single parents is increasing. Single-parent households headed by women are more disadvantaged than those managed by fathers. Families with only the mother present form the largest proportion of all of the various types of families in poverty (Gongla & Thompson, 1987).

CHARACTERISTICS OF EMPLOYMENT

Employment is closely tied to the economic fortunes of single-parent women. Spitze (1988) called for investigation of the conditions under which women's employment may have positive outcomes for them and their families, especially among single parents. Researchers have tended to focus on two-parent families and have neglected the consequences of employment for single parents. Yet, single-parent women are more likely to be in the labor force than their married peers. An objective of this chapter is to examine both subjective and objective consequences dimensions of work on psychological distress. We investigate the extent to which deficits attributed to single parents foster depressive symptoms and low self-concept and the degree to which time spent at work, gender-role attitudes, and social support may mitigate psychological distress. Research suggests that psychological distress is more prevalent among single individuals, with the possible exception of never-married women, than among married couples (Keith, 1989). Divorced persons have significantly more depressive symptoms than those who remain married (Menaghan, 1985). A further objective is to compare the relative importance of characteristics of employment, finances, and attitudes toward gender roles in fostering self-concept and depressive symptoms among employed mothers who are married and those who are single.

Brandwein et al. (1974) identified economic, authority, domestic, and emotional family functions as areas of difficulty for female single parents. Although the economic and domestic arenas are particularly stressful for single parents, two-job families, as noted in chapter 3, also experience strain and overload as they set about to reconcile the demands of homemaking and employment. Some of the demands associated with employment and domestic activities common to both single-parent and married women may be associated with psychological distress. In this chapter, we begin by comparing characteristics of employment, finances, and gender-role attitudes of the two groups of mothers. Keeping in mind the deficits attributed to the single-parent family, we then examined how factors pertaining to employment and finances differentially affected the well-being of both groups of women.

Finances and Psychological Well-Being

Undoubtedly, both single-parent and married women can anticipate some shared conflicts between employment and family activities. But other factors such as economic status may differentially impact the mental health of married and unmarried women. Not only do single parents experience greater financial deprivation (Gongla & Thompson, 1987), but marginal economic resources may foster greater depression among the unmarried (Pearlin & Johnson, 1977). Menaghan (1985) found no support for the social-selection perspective that the divorced are more depressed prior to the dissolution of the marriage. Rather, their greater depression was accounted for by a decline in their standard of living, increased economic difficulties, and the somewhat less intimate social support that they experienced prior to the end of the marriage (Menaghan, 1985). Buehler, Hogan, Robinson, and Levy (1985–1986) observed that the major role shift for mothers in the postdivorce period was in their becoming the primary economic provider. Those who were better educated and employed full-time had stronger ties to the labor market, indicating that education was a resource drawn on during the time of transition.

It has been observed that the economic strength of the two-parent family is denied to both male and female single parents (Brandwein et al., 1974). Women especially experience diminished economic well-being following the loss of a spouse. A common response to financial hardship is for divorced women to seek employment. In part because of their greater financial difficulties, work may be more salient in the lives of single-parent women than of their married peers and may figure more importantly in their mental health than for married women. Although the benefits of employment enjoyed by some may be entirely attributable to income earned from work, unmarried mothers without a marital partner may derive psychological benefits from social contacts in the workplace and additional role identity (Cohen et al., 1990). Previous research has indicated that the unmarried, particularly women, may define work differently in their lives than do the married (Keith, 1989; Veroff et al., 1981). Veroff et al. (1981) concluded that single men and women, more than their married peers, derived their social validity from work. Both previously married and never-married women found value fulfillment through work. Spending more time at work may reduce the amount of time available to meet nonwork obligations, but increased effort devoted to employment may represent greater commitment and may offer enhanced psychological benefits along with more income, all of which may diminish the potential for distress.

Work-Family Strain

Despite the fact that married employed women still retain primary responsibility for housekeeping tasks and child care, the absence of a spouse to assist with these functions has been described as a deficit of single-parent households. Presumably, the single mother will face even greater conflicts between the demands of work and home in the absence of a spouse who not only might contribute financially to the family but also might provide help with household tasks and family care.

Work-family role strain reflected in the interference between these two spheres might be especially prevalent in single-parent households; insofar as it is a factor in diminishing well-being, it will have further implications for these families. The notion of the chronic strain confronted by women in two-job and two-career families is much written about. But the majority of single female parents are vulnerable to many, if not more, of the same strains without the assistance of a partner to provide income or help with the household and children.

Brandwein et al. (1974) viewed the absence of a spouse to help with domestic functions of housekeeping and child care as a major deficit, although little is known about household management in single-parent families. Johnson (1986) described evidence of decreased social support available to the divorced single parent. Kin of the former spouse may be less available and/or there may be less assistance if the family does not approve of the divorce. Johnson found that the single mothers believed that they had sources of help available—the child's father, friends, and relatives. However, they did not believe that these sources would provide much help in managing responsibilities of the family. Although one-half of the women thought that they could receive nonfinancial help from the father, little assistance materialized. When help from the father was forthcoming, it tended to be provided early in the postdivorce period and was more often financial. Despite its presumed importance, however, support is not always reflected in increased adjustment of the divorced (Spanier & Hanson, 1981).

In single-parent households, it may be that more help is obtained from outside the home than in the two-parent family. In one model we investigated the degree to which the amount of help that women received with household activities from outside the home served as a buffer against distress. Even when help is secured from others outside the household, reallocation of tasks in the single-parent family may run counter to traditional gender-role attitudes.

ATTITUDES TOWARD GENDER ROLES

Clearly, employed single-parent women take on the major traditional male role of sole or primary provider in addition to carrying out domestic activities usually performed by women. In the situation in which women are called on to perform both traditional and less traditional roles, those with a wide repertoire of masculine and feminine behaviors from which to draw indeed may be advantaged. Women who hold more traditional attitudes toward the roles of women may identify most closely with the wife and mother roles, and in the single-parent family one of these traditional roles is no longer present. Nontraditional attitudes toward the potential satisfactions and rewards that may be derived from employment outside the family are resources as divorced women redefine their lives to encompass work roles outside the home (Brown & Manela, 1978). Conventional attitudes about the relationship of women to their home, family, and work especially may be a barrier to psychological well-being for those who assume the single-provider role in the family while at the same time managing the household.

Becoming or deciding to remain single whether widowed, divorced, or never married is not without a stigma, although that of the divorced may be the most negative (Keith, 1989). Etaugh and Malstrom (1981) observed that the married were regarded most favorably on more characteristics than were those in any unmarried group. Of the unmarried, however, the widowed were rated most positively and the divorced, who were evaluated as less dependable, more troubled, and less stable, were viewed the most negatively. As observed in chapter 7, the self-concept is formed through interaction with others and through interpretation of their responses. This process of self-definition, of course, is not limited to the marital relationship. If personal characteristics or situational factors do not provide a buffer and support, presumably the negative attitudes of others toward those who are single may erode the self-concept as disapproval is confronted (Keith, 1989). Whereas a divorced woman may experience the stigma of her marital dissolution, the married working mother of young children may still encounter resistance to her employment. Despite the involvement of married women in paid work, men continue to retain the recognition and responsibility for providing for the family (Thompson & Walker, 1989). For women in both situations, high regard for themselves may be a psychological resource to diminish distress. Consequently we considered self-concept in relation to depressive symptoms.

RESULTS

Characteristics of Employed Single and Married Mothers

First we investigated differences characteristic of employment, finances, attitudes toward gender roles, and mental health between single and married mothers. Corroborating other literature, married women reported somewhat fewer depressive symptoms ($\bar{X}$ = 2.25) than did single-parent women ($\bar{X}$ = 2.46; t = 2.43, p < .05), but single parents did not experience lower self-concept (t = .53, NS). Unmarried women were somewhat more committed to work ($\bar{X}$ = 3.26; married, $\bar{X}$ = 3.04; t = 2.03, p < .05) and they spent more hours in the labor force ($\bar{X}$ = 40 hrs; married, $\bar{X}$ = 29 hrs; t = 4.74, p < .001). The single women also confronted more work-family role strain ($\bar{X}$ = 2.62) than their married peers ($\overline{X}$ = 2.37; t = 2.08, p < .05). The women did not differ in the amount of satisfaction they derived from work-family tasks (t = .74, NS) although married women rated their performance in homemaking activities higher ($\overline{X}$ = 3.64) than the single parents ($\overline{X}$ = 3.34; t = 2.81, p < .01). The women held comparable attitudes toward female employment (t = .53, NS), whereas married women endorsed more traditional preferences for sharing household and work responsibilities ($\overline{X}$ = 3.66) than did single women ($\overline{X}$ = 3.45; t = 3.23, p < .01).

Multivariate Analyses of Depressive Symptoms

Separate multiple regression analyses of depression were conducted for single-parent and married women; variables with F values significant at the .10 level or above are presented in Table 8.1. The variables that were considered in the models were income, education, hours per week spent at work, commitment to work, work-family role strain, evaluation of self as a provider, and comparisons of financial and work situations with those of age and sex peers, self-concept, and attitudes toward gender roles.

Single Parents. As expected, nontraditional attitudes toward work-family gender roles were associated with fewer depressive symptoms among the single parents (r = .49, Table 8.1). Spending more time at work seemed to diminish psychological distress (r = −.37). Although higher income was linked to fewer depressive symptoms (r = −.25), it was not a significant determinant when other factors were considered. Women who worked more hours per week tended to have higher incomes (r = .20), but the relationship was not strong. Single parents who managed work-family strain more effectively were less depressed (r = .26), and a positive regard for self also reduced depressive symptoms (r = −.34). These factors explained 54 percent of the variance in depressive symptoms among single parents.

Evaluation of themselves as providers and commitment to work were not associated with distress when other factors were also considered, although greater commitment to work was correlated with less depression (r = −.36) at the zero-order level. The effect of work commitment on depressive symptoms may have been indirect through its association with work-family strain (r = −.37), in which women with greater commitment observed less interference between work and family.

As a test of the importance of social support available to and used by these single parents, in another model the amount of help that single parents received with home repairs, grocery shopping, cooking, laundry, caring for and training children, and yard work was included along with the other factors. Receiving more help from others was associated with less distress (r = −.31) but, when other factors were considered,

Table 8.1
Depressive Symptoms and Self-Concept of Single and Married Employed Mothers (Multiple Regression Analyses)

	Depressive Symptoms			
	Single-Parent Women N = 52		Married Women N = 87	
Characteristics	r	Beta	r	Beta
Gender-role attitudes	.49	.43**	.03	.08
Hours per week	-.37	-.37**	.18	.38**
Work-family strain	.26	.30**	.15	.03
Work commitment	-.35	.04	-.30	-.25**
Self-concept	-.34	-.22*	-.22	-.18*
Comparative financial situation	-.06	.09	-.27	-.37*
R^2	.54		.32	

	Self-Concept			
	Single-Parent Women N = 52		Married Women N = 87	
	r	Beta	r	Beta
Comparative financial situation	.19	.08	.25	.33**
Education	.28	.28*	.02	.10
Evaluation as earner	.30	.26*	.10	.16
R^2	.26		.13	

* $p < .10$
** $p < .05$

having been assisted by others did not have an independent effect on depressive symptoms. Furthermore, receiving more assistance was not associated with the amount of time women spent at work ($r = -.02$), although spending more time at work increased income somewhat ($r = .20$), which in turn seemed to prompt greater use of help from others ($r = .26$). Increased income was likely used to purchase services.

Married Women. There were some common correlates of depressive symptoms as well as some marked differences between the two groups of women. In contrast to single parents, married women who spent more time in the labor force were more distressed ($r = .18$). Of all of the factors included in the model, spending more time at work had the greatest effect on depressive symptoms of these married mothers (Table

8.1). In contrast to single parents, for whom work commitment had no direct effect on depressive symptoms, married women were less distressed if their work commitment was higher ($r = -.30$) and if they viewed their financial situation as comparatively favorable ($r = -.27$). As with their single counterparts, high self-concept seemed to be a resource that mitigated depressive symptoms for married women ($r = -.22$). These variables accounted for 32 percent of the variance in depressive symptoms.

Multivariate Analyses of Self-Concept

Separate multiple regression analyses of self-concept were conducted for single-parent and married women. The variables that were considered in the models were income, education, hours per week spent at work, commitment to work, evaluation of self as a provider, comparisons of financial and work situations with those of age and sex peers, and attitudes toward the roles of women. Only variables that were significantly associated ($p < .10$) with self-concept when others were considered simultaneously are presented in Table 8.1.

Single Parents. Only two of the factors were important to the self-concept of these single parents—educational level ($r = .28$) and evaluation of themselves as providers ($r = .30$). Having obtained more education and viewing one's performance as a provider more favorably contributed to positive self-regard. Less than one-half as much variance in self-concept was explained (26 percent) as was accounted for in depression.

Married Women. Only a positive comparison of their financial situation with that of other women their age fostered high self-concept among these employed married mothers with children still in the home ($r = .25$). Objective characteristics of employment (hours per week spent at work, income) had no direct effect on the self-regard of either group of women. Rather, income was associated with the comparison of their present financial situation ($r = .34$) by married women, which in turn was linked to self-concept. The model explained little of the variance in self-concept of employed married women, 13 percent.

CONCLUSIONS

These findings suggest factors that may facilitate the management of singleness, employment, and to a lesser extent, parenting. Background characteristics sometimes studied in relation to adjustment to divorce or widowhood are often not amenable to intervention. Clearly, events occurring during the marriage, length of marriage, or prior attitudes of children and/or spouse are not mutable, although their effects may linger. To some extent, personal characteristics that affected the distress of these single women may be open to change (gender-role attitudes, self-concept, time spent at work, and role strain).

Gender-role attitudes that may be targeted for change were especially important indicators of distress among the single parents. The assumption that nontraditional gender-role attitudes would facilitate well-being as both single parents and employed married women assumed more innovative work and family roles was only partially supported. Single women who believed that housekeeping and provider roles should be shared by males and females were less distressed when they found themselves in a situation in which they performed both.

Traditional gender-role ideologies markedly differentiate the activities of men and women, but the demands on a single parent usually ensure that less role differentiation will be possible. And traditional women may be less well prepared for the transition. Role transitions may be stressful, and adaptation to a role that is unconventional and ambiguous as well as new requires flexibility. When a newly assumed role exacts unconventional behavior that runs counter to long-held values, difficulties may be multiplied. The importance of gender-role attitudes in buffering distress suggests the need for individuals to know about the functions of these values in coping with less conventional family lifestyles.

The assumption that nontraditional gender-role attitudes would facilitate well-being as both single parents and employed married women assumed more innovative work and family roles was only partially supported. The more conventional attitudes reflected by married women again underscored the difficulty of maintaining egalitarian attitudes toward gender roles in a marital relationship. Furthermore, among these employed married women a nontraditional gender-role ideology failed to serve as a buffer against depressive symptoms, whereas single parents may have drawn strength from their less-traditional views about the work and family roles of women. For both groups of women self-concept was independent of gender-role attitudes.

Deficits in the economic sphere of the lives of single parents, reflected here in lower income, perceptions of less-favorable work and financial situations, and negative assessments of their abilities as providers, were less salient than other factors in determining depressive symptoms of single parents. More intense involvement in the workplace, for example, seemed to promote mental health independent of income. One of the benefits of greater involvement in work for the single-parent women may be feelings of independence and a source of gratification in addition to those from homemaking and child care.

Yet, spending more hours at work was not without its disadvantages because women who worked more experienced greater work-family role strain (r = .21). In turn, the strain from the interference between work and family was associated with depressive symptoms. These findings seem inconsistent, in that more time spent in the labor force was associated with strain but also with diminished depressive symptoms. It may be that the negative aspects of work reflected in overload and time constraints influenced work-family strain whereas positive outcomes of greater involvement in work (e.g., status enhancement, ego gratification) were conducive to less depression.

Presumably their spending more time at work might only confirm the image of single parents as less adept at child rearing than their married peers. Other analyses, however, indicated that these single parents who spent more time at work assessed their performance as parents more positively than women who were in the home more (r = .26). This may provide some support for the notion that the "quality" of time spent with children is more salient than the amount. For some, then, more intense involvement in the workplace enhanced perceived success in child rearing and insulated them somewhat against depression. As a whole, though, the lives of single parents, compared to those of married mothers, seemed more troubled; the former were more depressed, and they experienced more work-family role strain.

It has been assumed in the literature that part of the deficits of the single-parent family are centered in the absence of a partner to provide assistance with the domestic functions of the household. Our thinking was that receiving support from others outside the household in the form of instrumental assistance with tasks of daily living might mitigate the level of distress of single parents. Although receiving more assistance from others was negatively associated with depressive symptoms (r = −.31), a multivariate model tested did not have an independent effect on distress. Rather, what seemed to occur was that single parents with nontraditional gender-role attitudes accepted more help from others; thus, sustaining an egalitarian ideology lessened their distress. Once again this finding points to the salience of attitudes toward gender roles in the lives of single-parent women and suggests one possible point of intervention.

9

Food Behavior and Diet
Over the Life Stages

In chapters 3 and 5, the involvement of husbands and wives in work-family roles and some of the consequences of gender-linked activity were investigated. In this chapter, we focus specifically on food management activities in the family, the distribution of these tasks between spouses, and their linkage to relationships between marriage partners.

What were the outcomes for families who addressed food management in different ways? Why should we study the role of family activities surrounding food in a book on relationships and well-being? Although the task of food management is only one among an array of household activities in which families are involved, it is an important one for several reasons. (1) Food selection and preparation activities are among the most frequently recurring tasks for family members; a considerable number of hours per week are devoted to these by both full-time homemakers and employed women. (2) There is increasing interest among lay people and researchers in the specific relationship between food consumption, both type and amount, and its consequences for health. Therefore, food-related activities are important because of the link between dietary quality, health, and longevity. (3) The increase in two-job families has highlighted questions about the nature and allocation of household tasks, including food-related activities, in these households. There also are queries about the impact of female employment on the quality of the diet of family members. (4) There is also concern about physical appearance as it relates to weight and diet. (5) Finally, despite the centrality of food-related activities in the family, beyond consideration of the relationship between demographic characteristics, food habits, and diet, family food activities have been somewhat neglected by social scientists.

In this chapter, we examine the potential importance of food behavior and diet quality for well-being over the life stages. In the general evaluation of well-being across the life stages, food behavior and diet quality were important components of the investigation. What were the implications of food management in the household for the lives of the spouses we studied? To answer this question, four aspects of food behavior were examined.

The first concern was about who has responsibility for food management in the household; that is, who selects, purchases, and prepares food used by the family. The second issue examined the impact that wives' employment has on the quality of the diet of the marital partners. The third area of inquiry focused on food behavior and selected dietary changes of persons across the life stages. The fourth aspect of food behavior considered was the actual weight status of spouses in the different life stages. Each of these four general issues has implications for health and well-being and can inform us about the importance of life stages for food behaviors.

CONTROL OF FOOD IN THE FAMILY

Traditionally, women in Western culture have performed most of the housework roles, including food-related activities. There has been profound sex-typing and gender segregation, with the wife taking the main responsibility for household management and the husband preferring "functionally specific" work in the home that has clear and identifiable boundaries (Berk, 1985).

Recently, the assumption has been made that the dramatic increase of women participating in the labor force and the changing gender roles of men and women in society would result in greater sharing by husbands and wives of household tasks, including food-related activities. Sanjur (1982) suggests that the increasing number of homemakers who are employed outside the home has a strong impact on the participation of men in meal preparation. Helmick (1978) considers the notion of the housewife as "gatekeeper" for the family diet to be outdated. She notes that the mother is certainly no longer the gatekeeper to family food, if in fact she ever was. Speaking to the same issue, Fieldhouse (1986) suggests that whereas four decades ago Lewin (1943), in his study of food habits, was able to consider the housewife as the gatekeeper, with changes in family structure, social roles, and work opportunities, this can no longer be considered the case.

These assumptions concerning the changing roles of men and women in family food activities carry an intuitive logic. One would expect that a wife who is active in the work force would lessen her degree of participation in traditional homemaking activities, thus encouraging an increase in the degree of the husband's participation. The ramifications of such anticipated changes in participation are indeed intriguing and would suggest that some major restructuring is likely to occur in the behavior of men and women in food-related activities.

The effects of gender-role changes, however, may be more assumed than real. Generally it has been found that women continue to take the major responsibility for household tasks. Model (1981) found that domestic tasks are disproportionately carried out by women. She observed that wives were doing five times as much domestic work as their spouses and that, where husbands did contribute, they did so with the understanding that they were operating in "female territory." In a longitudinal study Nickols and Metzer (1982) showed that husbands of employed wives spent relatively little time in housework, including food-related activities, and this pattern persisted over the study period. Similarly, Fox and Nickols (1983) found that, while employed wives spent less time in the performance of household chores, this did not elicit a corresponding increase in time allocation to household activities by husbands. Food-related activities are still the domain of women and account for much of the time spent by wives in housework. Even though involvement of wives in food preparation is well established, the characteristics of family life stages suggest that there may be variation in the participation of spouses across the life stages. The objective in this analysis is to use the life-stage approach to examine participation of husbands and wives in food-related activities.

Food Activities in the Family

To determine participation of husbands and wives in food management activities in the home, we examined four elements of food selection and preparation: (1) identification of who in the family had the major responsibility for decisions about food selection, (2) the normative expectations of who should take the responsibility for food preparation, (3) identification of who actually prepared food for family consumption, and (4) the effect of food activities in the home on marital interaction patterns. Consideration of all four areas provides a comprehensive view of the role of husbands and wives in family food activities.

Decision Making about Food

Couples at each of the four life stages were asked a series of questions to determine their participation in food selection and preparation and their attitudes toward food activities in the home. Three questions were asked in order to measure the "gatekeeper" functions of the decisions and activities regarding selection of food for the family meals: (1) "Who usually makes the decision about what food items to purchase?" (2) "Who usually makes the decision about the amount of money spent on food?" (3) "Who usually does the grocery shopping in your family?" Responses included: (1) Husband always, (2) Husband more than wife, (3) Husband and wife about the same, (4) Wife more than husband, and (5) Wife always.

Expectations about Food Activities

To determine normative expectations for food behavior, partners were asked, "Please indicate who should do the cooking in the family." To determine actual food behavior in the home, respondents were asked, "Who usually does the cooking in the family?" Response categories for the normative and behavioral questions were the same as those used for decision making, ranging from "Husband always" to "Wife always."

Disagreement about Food Activities

To measure the implications of participation in food management for marital interaction, both spouses were asked about disagreement about food preparation. "Please indicate how often, if ever, you and your husband/wife disagree about who does the cooking." Subjects responded using a five-point scale: (1) never, (2) seldom, (3) sometimes, (4) frequently, and (5) very frequently. Finally, respondents were asked for their perception of the fairness of their own participation in food preparation: "Should you increase or decrease your efforts in cooking to make your marriage relationships more fair for both of you?" Response categories were: (1) decrease effort a great deal, (2) decrease effort somewhat, (3) present effort is fair, (4) increase effort somewhat, and (5) increase effort a great deal. In a separate question, subjects were also asked whether their partners should increase or decrease their efforts in cooking.

Food Activities Across the Life Stages

Table 9.1 presents a descriptive analysis of the perceived level of involvement of husbands and wives in family food activities. The data reported are mean scores for the ordinal measures of food activity. Examining the gatekeeping issues of who determines the type of food entering the home, we found that for each life stage both spouses observed that wives took the major responsibility for deciding which foods to purchase and how much money to spend on food. In addition, both

Table 9.1
Husbands' and Wives' Food Roles in the Home (Mean Scores)

Family Life Stages

Food Roles	Husbands				Wives			
	Stage 1 N = 85	Stage 2 N = 88	Stage 3 N = 82	Stage 4 N = 81	Stage 1 N = 85	Stage 2 N = 88	Stage 3 N = 82	Stage 4 N = 81
Who decides food purchases	4.1	4.0	4.0	3.6	4.2	4.0	4.0	3.8
Who decides money spent on food	3.9	3.8	3.9	3.7	3.9	3.8	3.9	3.7
Who does the grocery shopping	4.2	3.9	4.2	3.6	4.3	4.1	4.0	3.4
Who should cook	4.0	4.1	4.2	4.2	4.0	4.2	4.2	4.3
Who does cook	4.2	4.4	4.4	4.4	4.3	4.3	4.4	4.4

Mean scores are based on the following response categories: 1 = husband always, 2 = husband more than wife, 3 = husband and wife about the same, 4 = wife more than husband, 5 = wife always.

husbands and wives believed that wives were more involved in grocery shopping.

Husbands and wives both assumed that wives should do most of the cooking. Responses to the question of who actually does the cooking indicated that husbands and wives believed that wives performed the majority of cooking in the home, with husbands sharing only occasionally in that activity. Thus, for the subjects studied, there was a shared perception that wives should be responsible for most of the food preparation in the home.

Analysis of variance tests were conducted to determine if there were differences between the observations of husbands and wives. These tests showed no significant differences in the views of husbands and wives for any of the activities. Husbands and wives at each life stage agreed about who should and who did conduct most of the food-related activities and made most of the decisions in the household. However, there were significant differences between life stages for the three food activities: decisions about food purchases (F = 12.07, $p < .001$), responsibility for shopping (F = 17.76, $p < .001$), and who should prepare the food (F = 4.62, $p < .01$). Life-stage differences for decisions about food purchases and grocery shopping probably were due to the greater involvement of retired husbands (Stage 4) in these activities. Life-stage differences in the normative expectation of who should prepare food were attributable to a stronger perception by younger wives than older wives that husbands should be more involved in food preparation. Life stage was not a factor in the other food-related activities. There were no significant interaction effects between sex and life stage for food activities.

A one-way analysis of variance was used to determine the effect of employment status of the wife on food-management attitudes and behaviors. Forty-three percent of the women in the sample were in the work force. Mean score differences are shown in Table 9.2. In only a few cases were there significant differences between wives who were employed outside the home and wives who were not. For example, younger wives (Stages 1 and 2) who were employed expected their husbands to take more responsibility for cooking. Likewise, compared with wives who were full-time homemakers, employed wives in Stages 2 and 3 felt that their husbands were actually taking a greater role in cooking. The youngest employed wives expected greater husband involvement, but they believed that actual participation of their partner was not significantly different from that in households where women were not employed outside the home.

Perceptions of husbands of employed and nonemployed wives matched those of their wives. Husbands whose wives worked outside the home tended to be only modestly more involved in household food

Table 9.2
Effects of Employment Status of Wife on Food Activities of Husbands and Wives (One-way Analyses of Variance)

	Stage 1		Stage 2		Stage 3		Stage 4	
	E N = 40	NE N = 45	E N = 47	NE N = 41	E N = 48	NE N = 33	E N = 10	NE N = 72
Who decides food purchases?								
Husband	4.0	4.1	3.8	4.1*	3.9	4.2	3.6	3.6
Wife	4.15	4.3	3.8	4.2	3.9	4.1	3.8	3.7
Who decides money spent on food?								
Husband	3.9	3.9	3.6	3.9	3.9	4.1	4.3	3.6
Wife	3.9	3.9	3.7	4.0	3.9	4.1	3.6	3.7
Who does shopping?								
Husband	4.0	4.3	3.8	4.1	4.0	4.4	4.1	3.5
Wife	4.2	4.4	3.9	4.2	3.9	4.2	4.4	3.3
Who should cook?								
Husband	3.8	4.2***	4.0	4.3*	4.0	4.4**	4.1	4.2
Wife	3.7	4.2***	4.0	4.4**	4.1	4.3	4.5	4.3
Who does cooking?								
Husband	4.1	4.4*	4.1	4.6***	4.2	4.6**	4.4	4.2
Wife	4.2	4.4	4.1	4.6***	4.2	4.7***	4.4	4.4

Family Life Stages

E = Employed wife
NE = Non-employed wife

* p < .05
** p < .01
*** p < .001

activities than husbands of nonemployed wives. In all but the oldest groups, there were significant differences in involvement in food activities between husbands of employed wives and husbands whose wives were full-time homemakers. Husbands in two-job families felt they should get more involved in cooking than husbands in single-earner families. Within the life-cycle groups, husbands of employed wives reported they were significantly more involved in food preparation than husbands whose wives were full-time homemakers.

We found little evidence to support the belief that changing gender roles related to food introduced conflict into the marital relationship. Over 85 percent of the subjects in each life-cycle group said they "never" or "seldom disagreed" over who should do the cooking. The majority of husbands and wives felt that the current efforts they spent on food activities were fair. For the limited disagreement about food-related activities that was observed, there was a general decline with advancing life stages. This was true for both spouses (F = 6.47, $p < .01$). The longer subjects were married, the less likely they were to experience disagreement about activities involving food.

Conclusions about Food Activities in the Home

Food-related activities clearly remained the domain of women in this sample. No significant differences were found between husbands and wives in their perception of gender-related food activities. There were, however, certain life-stage differences in food behaviors and perceptions. There was greater participation by retired husbands than by those in other life stages. The greater participation of older husbands may reflect increased amounts of time available to retired males for housework and related activities. Also, younger wives, more than those in later life stages, felt that husbands should be more involved in family food activities. This may reflect, to a modest extent, changing gender attitudes that may eventually redefine a portion of the wives' roles in food preparation.

The conclusion that must be drawn from these data is that the employment status of the wife had little effect on food activities in the home. Both normative and behavioral assessments by the spouses indicated that wives should and did take most of the responsibility for the selection and preparation of food. The most notable exceptions to this were the expectations of younger couples and the actual involvement of older couples in cooking. The younger couples perhaps reflect the ideal, whereas the middle-aged couples demonstrate the most prevalent practice. But here again, differences were relative. The majority of wives, even though they were employed, still expected and were expected by husbands to assume most of the responsibility for the decisions and activities regarding food. Thus, the assumption that the employment of the homemaker outside the home might increase the participation of men in meal preparation and other food decisions was not supported.

The data suggested that the gender-role changes in contemporary American society (Lopata, Barnewalt & Norr, 1980) had not resulted in a major restructuring of food management in the families studied. Whereas these findings may reflect a regional artifact, the data were consistent with research on other household activities in which women continue to take major responsibility for tasks in the home.

In summarizing the research on husbands' contributions to household activities Berk (1985:9–10) noted:

Although husbands of employed wives and fathers with young children seem to participate in household labor at higher levels than husbands in different circumstances, the practical significance of that participation is debatable. A strong case can be made for concluding that the minimal participation of husbands in household labor and child care (relative to that of wives) is virtually constant although there is still much to learn. . . . The overall descriptive picture is difficult to refute, wives are responsible for and accomplish most household labor. Husbands may be pressed into service as secondary sources of intermittent labor, but they remain the primary beneficiaries of household service.

Hartmann (1981) makes the point even more strongly by suggesting that the contribution of husbands to housework is "rather small, selective, and unresponsive, and may thereby be a net drain on the family's resources of household time—they may require more housework than they contribute." This pattern appears to be fairly consistent, with only minor variations for social class, race, and age. Despite its cultural impact, because of attention by the mass media and scholarly research, a family in which both partners work and in which there is an egalitarian sharing of household labor is extremely rare. Gender equality is not the standard practice.

The reasons for the persistence of this traditional pattern in the face of major social changes may be found in the weight of tradition and economic imperatives. O'Kelly and Carney (1986) suggest four reasons for the continued dominance of women in household labor. First, the wife is likely to be better trained in domestic tasks because of gender-role socialization in childhood and adolescence socialization into the gender division of labor. This makes it easier for some wives to do the work, and spouses therefore fall back on traditional gender patterns. Second, the rest of society continues to place the responsibility for domestic tasks on the wife. Women may be blamed if there is a breakdown in the operation of the home. Third, employers have been less tolerant of family demands that interfere with male employment than with female employment. It is more acceptable for a woman to be absent because of a sick child than it is for a man. Fourth, the occupations of women are likely to be less prestigious and to pay less than those of men; therefore, if work is to be disrupted, it is most likely to be that of women.

The results of this study have important implications for nutrition education. That men in intact families take little direct responsibility for food selection and preparation suggests that nutrition education for improved health-status efforts could be directed in two distinct and opposite directions.

On the one hand, nutrition education may focus on the female audience. If resources are limited, it makes sense to target narrowly to boost the benefit-cost ratio. Although there is a small male audience for food management (food shopping and preparation), especially among the youngest and oldest life stages in intact families and perhaps among divorced or single male households, it remains a minor part of all family food management audiences. This is not to say that males are inept in household food-management tasks or uninterested. They simply are not the ones attending to major food activities within the family on a regular basis. Thus, targeting the females may permit greatest impact on well-being.

On the other hand, targeting males could increase the impact of educational efforts by broadening food-related interests among family members. An assumption of much nutrition education is that behavioral change is more likely to occur when all family members are involved, not just the gatekeeper. Communication of nutrition information within a family affects use of this information (Hertzler & Schulman, 1983). This study did not assess communication among family members concerning food roles, except in the area of conflict. But as Hertzler and Vaughan (1986) reported, there is often little food and nutrition information being shared in families, and therefore strategies may need to be designed so that information reaches all family members. Studies of attitudes and interests in diet and heart disease have shown males much less likely than females to be concerned (Kline & Terry, 1986). Thus, nutrition-education efforts targeted at males may actually enhance impact by bringing a supporting actor onto the stage of family food activities.

FEMALE EMPLOYMENT AND QUALITY OF DIETS OF HUSBANDS AND WIVES

While it has been demonstrated that wives' employment did not have a significant effect on the control of food activity in the home, a related question is "Does wives' employment have an influence on the quality of the diet of the marital partners?" Several themes in popular and social-science literature have focused on the difficulties that may occur when men and women attempt to allocate time between work and family. As noted in chapter 3, investigations of the consequences of employment of both husbands and wives generally have tended to emphasize deficits, including its effects on diet, that work outside the home may create for the individual, the family, or the marital relationship.

Few dietary or food-selection studies have considered the potential influence of women's employment on food choices in the household. One study examined the interest in and concern about nutrition by working mothers (Swanson-Rudd, Fox, Crumley, Doyle, Johnson & Nerull, 1983) and found general agreement by the women that their families were being adequately fed.

The limited research examining the relationship between health and women's employment indicates employed women experience better health than nonemployed women; however, that could be the effect of self-selection (healthier women go to work, sicklier women stay home) or the effect of greater life satisfaction. Although diet is a vital component of health, no serious attention has been paid the influence of women's employment on quality of diet among household members.

In this section we examine nutrient density as an indicator of diet quality of the diets of employed and homemaker women and their husbands. Are the diets of homemaker women higher in nutrient density than the diets of employed women, and are the diets of men with homemaker wives of higher nutrient density than the diets of men with employed wives?

Nutrient density was determined through the use of a food-frequency checklist of 120 foods. Respondents were asked to indicate how often they consumed each food and beverage item, and they could respond with daily, weekly, monthly, or yearly frequencies. No time frame was defined for responses. Respondents were simply asked to indicate present usual intake. Using three-dimensional food models, interviewers asked respondents to estimate usual serving sizes. Based on frequencies and usual serving sizes reported, nutrient contributions of the 120 foods were calculated on a daily basis and totalled to give an estimate of daily intake of calories and sixteen nutrients (protein, fat, saturated fat, monounsaturated fat, polyunsaturated fat, cholesterol, vitamin A, ascorbic acid, thiamin, riboflavin, preformed niacin, calcium, phosphorus, iron, sodium, potassium). Nutrient density is expressed as amount of nutrient per 1000 kilocalories.

The instrument was pretested for reliability. A test-retest technique with sixty young married women resulted in correlation of 0.64 to 0.87 between the two intake periods for specific nutrients.

Did women's diets differ based on employment outside the home? There were no significant differences in nutrient density of diets of homemaker versus employed women at any of the four stages in the life course examined.

Nutrient density of men's diets was not consistently higher or lower depending on whether the wife was a homemaker or employed outside the home. In neither the youngest family nor the middle-aged empty-nest families were there statistically significant differences in nutrient density for any of the sixteen nutrients between men with employed or homemaker wives. Husbands in maturing families (Stage 2) with an employed wife reported a diet significantly less nutrient-dense in vitamin A than husbands with a homemaker wife ($t = 63.78$, $p < .05$).

Among elderly couples, diets of husbands of employed versus home-maker wives differed on two nutrients. Husbands of employed wives consumed fewer grams of fat per 1000 kcals than did husbands of home-maker wives ($t = 6.70$, $p < .05$). At the same time husbands of employed wives reported a more iron-dense diet than did husbands of homemaker wives ($t = 17.35$, $p < .05$). Despite statistical significance, these differences are small in the context of the total diet and probably of little nutritional significance.

We made 128 comparisons, comparisons of sixteen nutrients each for employed and homemaker women in four household types and comparisons of sixteen nutrients each for husbands of employed and homemaker wives in four household types. Among the 128 comparisons we found only three in which nutrient density differed between households with a full-time homemaker or a wife employed outside the home. It is clear that the nutrient density of diets of employed women was not higher than that of diets of homemaker women. Furthermore, the diets of the husbands of employed women were not of lower nutrient density than diets of husbands of full-time homemakers.

There is a concern over the impact of the employment of both spouses on the family and the marital relationship and the health status of the family. However, in this analysis the employment status of the wife did not have an appreciable influence on the quality of diets of marriage partners in any of the life-cycle stages. While a common assumption would be that diet quality would suffer because of women's employment, this was not found to be the case for the respondents in our study.

FOOD HABITS ACROSS THE LIFE STAGES

Food habits of subjects in the four life stages were categorized into the following activities: meals and snacks eaten, time spent preparing foods, husband's involvement in preparing meals, and recent changes in food habits. These activities can have subtle influences on the quality of diets of individuals and by implication on health status. Information on these different aspects of food practices will be useful in understanding food behavior at each life stage and how these activities vary across the different stages. The findings are reported in Table 9.3. In these analyses, the habits of single parents are considered as well.

Meals Eaten Per Day

Couples indicated the number of meals they consumed daily. An attempt was made in this assessment to establish differences between life stages in the regularity of meal patterns. The young and middle-aged husbands and wives were relatively consistent in eating an average of 2.5 meals per day. The elderly married couples, however, were more regular in their meal patterns, eating on the average close to three meals per day. The greater meal regularity of the elderly may reflect their life stage, in which there may be fewer activities and commitments that would compete with the traditional pattern of three meals a day.

Snacks Eaten Per Day

Respondents were asked how many snacks they consumed daily. For some the consumption of snacks may suggest questionable food behavior that may compromise diet quality through the excessive intake of calories and the disruption of more regularized eating patterns. As with meals eaten per day, there was a clear distinction between the young and middle aged as compared to the elderly in the number of snacks eaten each day. Couples in the two youngest groups and single parents ate an average of 1.5 to two snacks a day. The middle-aged couples ate fewer snacks, an average of 1.2, whereas the elderly ate only one snack or less per day. In eating regular meals and avoiding snacks the elderly demonstrated more appropriate habits than those at other life stages.

Time Spent Preparing Food

The amount of time spent per day on food preparation by women reflected family size with the exception of the oldest families. The greatest amount of time in food preparation was spent by the wives in the first life stage. The youngest women spent an average of a little over one and one-half hours per day. The time spent preparing meals decreased over the life stages except for the oldest wives, who spent on the average 1 hour and 50 minutes per day. This may reflect the greater amount of time that older women had available for various household activities.

Table 9.3
Food Habits of Husbands and Wives in Different Family Life Stages

	Stage 1		Single Parent Female N = 78	Stage 2		Stage 3		Stage 4	
	Husbands N = 85	Wives N = 85		Husbands N = 88	Wives N = 88	Husbands N = 81	Wives N = 81	Husbands N = 82	Wives N = 82
Meals eaten per day (mean)	2.5	2.5	2.3	2.5	2.5	2.7	2.6	2.9	2.9
Snacks eaten per day (mean)	1.9	1.6	1.5	1.4	1.5	1.2	1.3	.9	.9
Time spent by women preparing food (minutes)		106	88		94		84		112
Percentage of husbands' involved in food preparation	35%			32%		39%		30%	
Percentage positive change in food habits	22%	39%	49%	23%	41%	25%	25%	25%	25%

Husbands' Involvement in Food Preparation

The findings reported in Table 9.3 indicate that approximately a third of the husbands across the different life stages become involved in meal preparation. Furthermore, the amount of time they spent was considerably less than that of the wife, ranging from 55 minutes per day for families with older children to 27 minutes for empty-nest families. As reported earlier, the wife was clearly the main food preparer; however, a sizeable number of husbands did become actively involved in meal preparation and spent an average of a half-hour per day on food preparation.

Changes in Diet Pattern

The respondents at each life stage were asked whether they had changed their eating habits lately and, if so, what was the nature of the change. Of the total sample, 30 percent indicated a recent change in their food habits. Of these individuals, 97 percent indicated they made a positive dietary change such as eating less sugar, fat, salt, or fried foods and consuming fewer calories.

In examining the differences across the life stages, it was found that a higher percentage of younger wives had made positive changes in their diet than had the wives or husbands in any other group. Among husbands across all groups and wives in the two older life stages, approximately 25 percent changed compared to approximately 40 percent of the younger wives. Among the married, the two youngest groups of wives were most active in taking steps to improve their diets. Single-parent women most often had improved their diets (49 percent).

WEIGHT CONTROL

Concern about being overweight has become a national pastime. Whether this concern is prompted by health problems or concern for physical appearance and attractiveness, individuals have shown an intense, albeit sometimes flighty, interest in weight control and what constitutes ideal weight. Medical studies have demonstrated a clear relationship between overweight and obesity and a variety of physical illnesses, especially cardiovascular problems. Evidence is conclusive that obesity has adverse effects on health and longevity, and it is clearly associated with hypertension, hypercholesterolemia, and non–insulin-dependent diabetes mellitus. With this public awareness of the link between diet and health and wellness has come a growing concern for health education. The emphasis is on self-responsibility for the adoption of a healthful life-style, defined by an appropriate diet and maintaining reasonable weight. In the discussion of physical well-being it would not be inappropriate to suggest that the most obvious nutritional problem in the United States at the current time is overweight. Recent estimates suggest that approximately 40 percent of American adults are overweight to the extent that it may harm health.

The number-one cause of death in the United States is heart disease. Although the etiology is multifactorial, the majority of health scientists agree that diet is a major factor. In December 1984, the National Institutes of Health convened a consensus panel that, after reviewing the evidence, concluded that there was no longer any question that the American diet was a significant contributor to high mortality from heart disease (NIH, 1985). In addition, there is valid evidence that the American diet plays a role in many chronic diseases such as diabetes, certain cancers, and hypertension. Furthermore, the National Cancer Institute estimates that 80 percent of all cancer cases are due to life-style behaviors such as diet, occupation, and smoking (NCI, 1982).

This section will examine the weight status of the couples in the different life stages. Our analyses of weight status will focus on differences (1) between life stages and (2) between married and single-parent women. Weight status was based on weight, height, frame size, and sex. The weight measure presented in chapter 4 specified the percentage of persons who were overweight or underweight. In this chapter, the percentage who were overweight or underweight was codified to represent four general weight categories: underweight = 10 percent or more under ideal weight; ideal weight = not more than 10 percent overweight or underweight; overweight = between 10 percent and 20 percent overweight; obese = 20 percent or more overweight.

The weight status of the couples at different life stages and single-parent women is presented in Table 9.4. The percentage underweight was relatively stable over the life stages, with only slightly higher percentages for the elderly. For those subjects at ideal weight there was an interesting, albeit modest, trend. Whereas the majority of respondents were in the ideal weight category, there was a tendency for the percentage of males in this category to increase over the life stages; there was an opposite tendency for the percentage of females at ideal weight to decrease over the life cycle, with the greatest drop to occur between the Stage 1 and Stage 2 females. There was a slightly lower percentage of single-parent females at ideal weight than of their married counterparts.

In the overweight and obese category, which is of greatest concern because of the implications for physical well-being, the percentage over ideal weight (overweight + obese) was similar to national estimates. Thirty-seven percent of subjects at all life stages were either overweight or obese. National estimates are that 40 percent of the population is

Table 9.4
Weight Status of Couples in Different Family Life Stages and of Single-Parent Women

| | Stage 1 | | Stage 2 | | Stage 3 | | Stage 4 | | Single-Parent Female |
	Husbands N = 85	Wives	Husbands N = 88	Wives	Husbands N = 81	Wives	Husbands N = 82	Wives	N = 78
Underweight	6%	11%	4%	9%	6%	10%	15%	14%	15%
Ideal weight	58%	55%	60%	47%	62%	49%	67%	44%	42%
Overweight	17%	17%	18%	17%	20%	23%	9%	22%	13%
Obese	19%	17%	18%	27%	12%	18%	10%	20%	30%

overweight. Examining the difference between men and women in these two overweight categories, 31 percent of men were over ideal weight compared to 42 percent of the female respondents. Across the life course the pattern of overweight and obesity for men was relatively stable, with a decline at the later life stages. Women in some categories were also relatively stable in couples over the life stages, with the exception of Stage 2 female respondents and single-parent females.

In examining weight status we found male and female respondents at health risk because of being overweight in proportion to the population at large. Life-stage differences suggest a modest shift of males away from overweight to ideal weight and a parallel modest shift of women from ideal weight to overweight. The key factor in this change is the weight gain associated with childbearing.

The greatest deviation from the weight pattern across the life stages is for females in maturing families and single-parent females. These two groups had 27 percent and 30 percent respectively in the obese weight category. By definition these life stages represent the childbearing years and therefore suggest that the overweight found for these two groups may in part be a function of childbearing.

CONCLUSION

In this chapter we examined various aspects of food behavior over the family life stages. Food behavior is salient as a health condition and warrants consideration in a study of well-being over the family life stages. We found that wives continue to take major responsibility and control for food decisions, purchases, and preparation. Furthermore, the employment of wives outside the home did not have much impact on food purchases and preparation. Generally, wives who worked outside the home had the same level of responsibility as wives who were homemakers. We also found that the quality of diet was not diminished by wives' employment outside the home. Both wives who were employed and homemakers had similar-quality diets and so did their husbands. Therefore, employment of wives outside the home did not change the pattern of wife as gatekeeper nor have a negative effect on diet quality.

We also found that couples in the older life stages had more stable food habits and that a higher percentage of younger wives had made positive changes in their diet. Weight status of couples changed only slightly over the family life cycle, with wives showing an increase in the overweight and obese categories over family life stages. Single parents were most often overweight, but they were making positive changes in their dietary habits.

10

A Concluding Glimpse of Families Over the Life Stages

Our findings are not definitive, but rather another step in successive attempts to understand personal characteristics and circumstances that affect responses to the demands of work and family and, finally, well-being. For much of this book, a guiding question has been, "How did factors that influence responses to work and family relationships vary by life stages?" Were situations that prompted well-being comparable across the life stages? These issues were among our primary concerns. Our intent was not to test a theory of family development but rather to use the perspective as a framework in which to investigate correlates of family life stages (Aldous, 1990). Our work provides a glimpse of the lives of couples of various ages and in different family structures.

The concept of family life stages was selected because in a general way it represents the adjustments that partners have to make to each other and to other family members as they experience major role transitions and variation in needs, behavior, privileges, and responsibilities. Family life stages presuppose qualitative changes as the family matures. Each stage is distinct from the others because of the events and circumstances faced by the family at that particular time. Families in the same stage confront similar problems, which differ from those of previous stages and require different interaction patterns to address them.

The process of partners moving through life stages is a dynamic one as they identify and devise new means of approaching emergent demands. Our initial guiding framework suggested that adjustments and changes that spouses make in the various life stages will have implications for their activities and well-being. In this concluding chapter, we highlight some of the findings that address the importance of life stage as a correlate of the views, attitudes, and behavior of the individuals who were studied. Like much other research, issues that we have omitted may suggest the direction for future investigations.

What have we learned from these couples? How different was it to be a spouse in a younger partnership than in an older one? Because gender-role attitudes have been identified (chapter 1) as having undergone significant change and because their shift represents a major trend in American society, we begin by summarizing how the implications of these views varied by life stage. It is assumed that gender-role attitudes may be reflected in the ways in which families meet demands and make decisions that are characteristic of the various stages.

THE LONG REACH OF GENDER-ROLE ATTITUDES

Gender-role attitudes were important correlates, if not antecedent factors, in influencing the ways in which some of the events and activities were articulated in these families. The prominence of gender-role attitudes especially in the involvement of spouses in feminine tasks warrants comment.

First, whether gender-role attitudes were modern or more traditional was linked to the household involvement of husbands and wives in most of the life stages. Thoughts about gender roles were especially salient in predicting the division of labor in feminine tasks in younger families. Both husbands and wives acted on their traditional or modern views, although the division of labor tended to be organized along traditional lines in the families studied. As suggested in other research (Antill & Cotton, 1988), traditional wives spent more time on feminine tasks and, correspondingly, nontraditional husbands did more housework. An exception was the lack of importance that gender-role attitudes had for activities in the oldest families. Older men were more involved than younger men in housekeeping, but their behavior was not directly affected by their gender-role attitudes, their own employment status, or that of their wives. Thus, the view that ideology is a critical dimension in reducing the traditional division of labor (Antill & Cotton, 1988) may warrant reconsideration if it is to be applied across the family life stages. It should be noted, however, that research has not always found that egalitarian beliefs are reflected in the distribution of family work (e.g., Crouter et al., 1987; Thompson & Walker, 1989).

In the families that we studied, though, views of gender roles were important in determining the feminine activities of middle-aged and younger husbands and wives and for masculine activities among women in the early and middle life stages. For all of the greater cross-gender participation of men in the oldest families, it was independent of their attitudes. Participation in these activities may be explained more by time available than by ideology. For the majority of families—more than time available, women's employment, resources, or attitudes—gender accounts for the allocation of family work (Thompson & Walker, 1989).

Another view of the relationship between gender-role attitudes and family life stage was provided by the study of marital role congruence. In the typology of marital role congruence, marriages were profiled by determining whether spouses held modern or traditional attitudes and whether they maintained congruent or incongruent views. Family life stage was clearly linked with patterns of marital role congruence. Younger families with children in the home were more likely than middle-aged and older spouses to hold congruent, nontraditional attitudes. More than their younger counterparts, middle-aged and older families maintained a pattern in which the husband was traditional and the wife was modern. In some research (Bowen & Orthner, 1983), this incongruent pattern has been found to foster difficulty for spouses although incongruent attitudes were not especially troubling to the partners that we studied. Regardless of life stage, the congruent modern and congruent traditional patterns were differentiated from one another. Life stage made a difference in one of the factors that distinguished among the patterns of marital role congruence: employment of the wife differentiated between congruent modern and congruent traditional young spouses. By middle age, wives' employment no longer distinguished between modern and traditional spousal patterns. Employment may be defined differently by younger women. The multiple roles of parent of younger children, worker, and spouse and the gender-role attitudes of partners likely reciprocally influenced one another so that congruent attitudes between spouses probably made it easier for young women to manage the demands of work and family.

Involvement in feminine activities differentiated between patterns across the life stages. Our evidence tends to highlight the importance of gender-role attitudes and actual behavior in the household in describing the contemporary marital patterns that were evolved by families. The strength of gender-role attitudes was demonstrated by their influence on activities both within and outside the household (i.e., involvement in feminine tasks by both sexes and in female employment). Contrary to theorizing, incongruent patterns did not seem to be linked with diminished psychological well-being nor did congruent views foster positive perceptions of circumstances. Patterns of contemporary marriages, in which female employment and financial responsibility were used to derive a typology, also were not associated with well-being. Being more modern, with both spouses contributing equally to family finances or conducting their lives traditionally, did not enhance self-concept or promote well-being among these partners. Life stage, however, was clearly a factor in the variation in some activities characteristic of the marital patterns. As suggested in chapter 1, life stages broadly demarcated activities and views of spouses within them.

Similarities between Partners

To discuss marital sex-role congruence and incongruence is to acknowledge that spouses do not always share attitudes or hold similar orientations toward issues that are thought to make a difference in how they may live their lives. This raises the following questions: "To what extent did husbands and wives maintain comparable perceptions of their relationship, and did they enjoy similar levels of well-being?" "Did the similarity of partners' views differ by life stage?"

In addition to the demands and needs of each life stage that call for spouses' attention, there is also the factor that, as partners age, they are accumulating common experiences together. In the study of relationship development, it has been found that in intimate relationships there is a transformation of partners' attitudes, values, and beliefs, causing them to converge over time (Price & Vandenberg, 1980; Stephen, 1985). A key element in explaining increased similarity lies in the cognitive interdependence thought to develop between partners. A "circular-causal" model of relationship development may help account for increased similarity between partners (Levinger, 1983). As spouses interact, there is a mutual contamination of cognitive elements including values, beliefs, and attitudes. Persons' views of the world are subtly changed, altered, and recast as spouses communicate and make changes to accommodate each others' divergent views. The consequence of this process is the increased similarity between partners and the mutual construction of a shared system of meanings that define the partner relationship. If this theorizing is applied to the life stages, we might expect to find greater homogeneity in the views and attitudes of marital partners across the life stages.

Our findings that address the hypothesis that increasing similarity between partners will be found at the later life stages warrant comment because they generally failed to support this view. The following measures were used as evidence for this conclusion: two measures of attitudes toward gender roles, partners' assessments of their own performance in work-family tasks, satisfaction, disagreement, and two indices of well-being—role strain and depressive symptoms.

Contrary to the prediction of convergence, the oldest couples held the most heterogeneous views of their relationship, their well-being, and gender-role attitudes. On all but one of the indices, the oldest husbands and wives differed significantly. The framework of convergence suggests that close personal communication will lead to progressively greater disclosure and development of a shared couple reality. It may be that if assessments of basic beliefs about religion, politics, or other issues had been obtained, then the increased similarity between partners might have been observed. However, similarity did not follow from opportunities to develop cognitive interdependence and communication for these oldest spouses. They did not reconstruct their perceptions of circumstances in their lives toward greater similarity. A shared reality among older spouses was generally not observed, at least on the indices we studied. Unlike any of the younger groups, these oldest couples differed in their perceptions of the amount of disagreement between them and their spouses and in the amount of satisfaction derived from involvement in work-family activities.

It might be expected that the oldest families would have the most time for communication as well as historically having had an opportunity to shape and reinterpret their reality as a couple. The kinds of measures that were available simply may not take into account the changes that come about in spousal relationships with the retirement of one or both members of the family or the influence of shifts in gender-role orientations in later life. The data modestly suggest that "his" and "her" marriages may persist into the latest life stages and that the bifurcation may even be the most prevalent in those groups. The greater heterogeneity observed in the older population as a whole may not be mitigated entirely even by the close communication thought to occur in a most intimate relationship.

Work and Well-Being

Role burdens are the subjective experiences that may accompany responsibilities (Verbrugge, 1987). Role burdens differentially affected the well-being of employed husbands and wives. Wives in dual-earner households were distressed and experienced greater role strain when their husbands also were burdened by greater interference between work and family and time demands. But husbands were not more strained by their wives' discomfort. This complements other research suggesting that women are more responsive to interpersonal concerns in marriage than are men (Thompson & Walker, 1989). Men in two-job families felt less strain if they evaluated their own and their spouses' earning capacities positively, but when their wives worked more hours, husbands had somewhat more negative evaluations of themselves as earners. Despite the efforts of their wives in the labor force, husbands retained both the recognition and the responsibility for the provider role. Consequently, for the husbands that we studied, concern about aspects of provision were distressing for those in two-job families.

The discomfort of wives reflected in their strain was less directly important to the husbands' well-being than the large amount of time that they spent at work. Wives, however, were not burdened by thoughts about the adequacy of family members as providers; rather, they were troubled by their husbands' role strain. Being affected by the role strain of a spouse was not sex-linked, however, because men in one-job families were also stressed when their wives felt overloaded. Rather, the role strain of men in two-job families seemed more responsive to both subjective and objective dimensions of finances (e.g., income and evaluation as a provider) than that of men in single-earner families. In summary, strain was especially more prevalent among the younger than the older dual-earner men. But age was a less important predictor of strain among employed women in two-job families and men in one-job families than it was for husbands in dual-earner households.

Strained and Unstrained Dual-Earner Families

In the majority of marriages, the subjective experiences and troubles of one spouse are thought to be inexorably intertwined with and reflect those of the other (Hinchcliffe et al., 1978). It might be expected then that spouses would be especially sensitive to the strains manifested by the other. Earlier, however, we observed that spouses may not share a commonly defined reality, and therefore we found a variety of patterns of strain among couples. Consequently, families ranged from those in which both spouses were highly strained to those in which one partner viewed work and their private life as overlapping and intrusive and the other did not observe interference between work and family activities. Still others managed their lives together so that neither of them was highly strained. But how did circumstances differ, especially for the polar types of families, the strained and unstrained?

Family life stage was strongly linked with patterns of strain of partners in dual-earner families. Lives of younger couples were more fraught with demands from employment and family members that resulted in a substantially greater likelihood that both partners would be strained. The interface between occupational and family demands was inharmonious and reflected in high strain for both partners in more than one-third of the young families compared to less than 10 percent of the middle-aged and older couples. This suggests that factors differentiating family life stages may have major input in fostering patterns characterizing strained and unstrained families.

Husbands and wives in strained families had different characteristics. Characteristics of husbands were more salient in differentiating between strained and unstrained families. In the most-strained families, younger husbands worked long hours, but they failed to realize greater job satisfaction despite their greater work commitment. These husbands were burdened by feelings of deprivation for being in a dual-earner family. In strained families, men who seemingly put the most into their work realized the fewest intrinsic benefits. Their wives shared the high level of strain, but the work characteristics and the burdens of husbands primarily dominated and differentiated strained from unstrained families. In summary, as a group, wives managed the most pronounced role strain, but when strain was studied as a family characteristic, it was the husbands' experiences that differentiated most clearly between harried and calmer families. In other instances in families, the preferences of husbands have been found to count more or to be more salient than those of wives (Hiller & Philliber, 1986).

Life Stage and Outcomes of Cross-Gender Role Behavior

Outcomes of involvement in cross-gender activities were linked to life stage. For example, well-being of the oldest spouses was most influenced by their own cross-gender involvement and that of their partner. The oldest spouses benefited from participation in gender-typed activities and were disadvantaged by involvement of their partner in cross-gender activities. These oldest spouses experienced more depressive symptoms when more nontraditional gender roles were practiced in their families. Moreover, across the life stages, nontraditional activities tended to foster greater disagreement between spouses. To carry out nontraditional practices was not without its costs for these families.

We, however, observed the importance of nontraditional gender-role attitudes as a resource against depressive symptoms among employed single-parent women. In many instances, it is necessary for single-parent women to engage in more cross-gender behavior and perhaps to act on and develop less-traditional attitudes. But nontraditional attitudes did not perform the same function for employed married mothers, although under certain conditions modern attitudes seem to reduce depression among married women (Mirowsky, 1985). Mirowsky has suggested the need to integrate research on equity, marital power, and depression. He observed that depression of women was diminished when they had more power and held less-traditional gender-role attitudes whereas depression of husbands was least when they had higher incomes. The gap between the optimum levels of equity for husbands and wives was greatest when men had high earnings and their wives held nontraditional gender-role attitudes.

LIFE STAGE, EQUITY, AND WELL-BEING

Fairness or equity in a marriage relationship may be a component of marital adjustment that often has not been taken into consideration. We observed that a high proportion of spouses believed there was equity in their marriage in general and in the performance of specific work-family roles, with the perception of equity tending to increase over the life stages. Moreover, those who experienced inequity more often believed it was in their favor rather than benefiting their partner. Wives, however, did not appraise their circumstances as favorably as did their husbands, especially the youngest and oldest wives, who felt more underbenefited in cooking and housekeeping than did other wives. Much as others have asked why wives with high levels of resources are not more dissatisfied with the division of labor and demand more assistance from their husbands (Spitze, 1988), we might ask why more wives do not feel underbenefited in their marriages. In long-term intimate relationships, less emphasis may be placed on the calculation of favors. In the instances of older spouses, the relationship has more of a history, during which time the situation may have seemed more equitable. For younger spouses, there is thought to be a future in which some repayment for feelings of being underbenefited may occur.

Much like disagreement between spouses, the experience of inequity was not without its costs. Marriage partners who were either underbenefited or overbenefited revealed more depressive symptoms than spouses who perceived equity. Being underbenefited in perhaps the most important relationship in the lives of many persons, and one that is not easily ended, may be especially disappointing and distressing. The underbenefited may feel victimized and progressively evaluate themselves negatively. But the self-regard of the overbenefited may not escape the influence of inequity. The overbenefited may feel guilt because of their more favored circumstances. Similar to the significance of outcomes of inequity, the tenor of self-evaluation that occurs in an intimate relationship also figures in well-being.

Unlike some of the characteristics studied in this book, evaluations of the self (self-concept) were not closely linked with life stage. The assessment of self-concept over the family life stages suggested a rather stable construction that did not necessarily increase or decrease in relation to the major role transitions that define life stages. Furthermore, the differences between husbands and wives that were found for some of the indices were largely absent for individuals' assessments of their self-concept. Moreover, what was important for psychological well-being was spouses' perception of their partners' evaluation of them. This underscores once again the interactive nature of the self. A disturbance in the self-view originating from the assumption that their partner had a low assessment of them led to a diminished sense of self-worth and subsequently contributed to depressive symptoms. Thus, low self-concept was conducive to depression, but so were the actual and perceived appraisals from someone with biographical significance for the partner. Actual and perceived appraisals from a significant other were doubly important because they defined the self-concept and because they had a direct effect on depressive symptoms. In this way the reaffirmation of the self, either positive or negative, clearly takes place in what Hinchcliffe et al. (1978) have called the crucible of marriage.

In chapter 5, we observed how life stage was linked with disagreement and evaluation of performance in work-family activities, gender-role attitudes, and household involvement of both men and women. Life stage was also a factor in perceptions of equity. Our research, then, has demonstrated several differences in the ways in which spouses responded to their work-family circumstances by life stage. The design, however, did not permit us to assess the age, period, and cohort effects that may have occurred. But we do know that in a general way the life stages that we employed seemed to distinguish between behavior of some family members. There were sex differences as well, although they were reflected not so much in differential observations of men and women about their lives as in the factors that seemed to foster particular outcomes of interaction or processes in the family.

Throughout, however, this research demonstrated the salience of the reciprocal nature of the marriage relationship. Whether in marriage the definition of the self is bolstered or diminished, whether attitudes are congruent or conflicting, whether the family is harried or peaceful, these circumstances in which a long-term intimate relationship is carried out have an extended reach leading to how the self is defined, how the relationship is regarded, and eventually how psychological well-being is experienced. Much of what happened to these partners occurred somewhat differently across the family life stages and sometimes differently for husbands and wives.

References

Abramson, L. Y., Seligman, M. E. P. & Teasdale, J. D. (1978). Learned help-lessness in humans: Critique and reformulation. *Journal of Abnormal Psychology*, 87, 29–74.

Ade-Ridder, L. & Brubaker, T. (1988). Expected and reported division of responsibility of household tasks among older wives in two residential settings. *Journal of Consumer Studies and Home Economics*, 12, 59–70.

Ade-Ridder, L. & Hennon, C. (Eds.). (1989). *Lifestyles of the Elderly*. New York: Human Sciences Press.

Aldous, J. (1990). Family development and the life course: Two perspectives on family change. *Journal of Marriage and the Family*, 52, 571–583.

Aldous, J. (1978). *Family Careers*. New York: John Wiley.

Alwin, D. F. & Hauser, R. M. (1975). The decomposition of effects in path analysis. *American Sociological Review*, 40, 37–47.

Anderson, E. & Leslie, L. (1989). Coping with stress: Differences among working families. In T. Miller (Ed.), *Stressful Life Events*. Madison, Wis.: International Universities Press.

Andrews, F. M. (Ed.). (1986). *Research on the Quality of Life*. Survey Research Center. Ann Arbor: University of Michigan.

Antill, J. & Cotton, S. (1988). Factors affecting the division of labor in households. *Sex Roles*, 18, 531–553.

Arendell, T. (1986). *Mothers and Divorce: Legal, Economic, and Social Dimensions*. Berkeley: University of California Press.

Aron, A. (1988). The matching hypothesis reconsidered again: Comment on Kalick and Hamilton. *Journal of Personality and Social Psychology*, 54, 441–446.

Austin, W. & Walster, E. (1974). Reactions to confirmations and disconfirmations of expectancies of equity and inequity. *Journal of Personality and Social Psychology*, 30, 208–216.

Bahr, S. & Peterson, E. (Eds.). (1989). *Aging and the Family*. Lexington, Mass.: Lexington Books.

Ballweg, J. A. (1967). Resolution of conjugal role adjustment after retirement. *Journal of Marriage and the Family*, 29, 277–281.

Barnett, C. R. & Nietzel, M. T. (1979). Relationship of instrumental and affectional behaviors and self-esteem in distressed and nondistressed couples. *Journal of Consulting and Clinical Psychology*, 47, 946–957.

Baruch, G. & Barnett, R. (1987). Role quality and psychological well-being. In F. Crosby (Ed.), *Spouse, Parent, Worker*. New Haven: Yale University Press.

Beck, A. T. (1974). The development of depression: A cognitive model. In R. J. Friedmann & M. M. Katz (Eds.), *The Psychology of Depression: Contemporary Theory and Research*. Washington, D.C.: V. H. Winston.

Beck, A. T. (1967). *Depression: Clinical, Experimental and Theoretical Aspects*. New York: Hoeber.

Bem, S. L. (1974). Measurement of psychological androgyny. *Journal of Consulting and Clinical Psychology*, 42, 155–162.

Benin, M. & Agostinelli, J. (1988). Husbands' and wives' satisfaction with the division of labor. *Journal of Marriage and the Family*, 50, 349–361.

Berardo, D., Shehan, C. & Leslie, G. (1987). A residue of tradition: Jobs, careers, and spouses' time in housework. *Journal of Marriage and the Family*, 49, 381–390.

Berger, C. E. (1973). Attributional communication situational involvement, self-esteem and interpersonal attraction. *Journal of Communication*, 23, 284–305.

Berger, P. & Kellner, H. (1964). Marriage and the construction of reality: An exercise in the micro sociology of knowledge. *Diogenes*, 46, 1–24.

Berk, S. F. (1985). *The Gender Factory: The Apportionment of Work in American Households*. New York: Plenum Press.

Berscheid, E., Dion, K., Walster, E. & Walster, G. W. (1971). Physical attractiveness and dating choice. A test of the matching hypothesis. *Journal of Experimental Social Psychology*, 4, 191–203.

Berscheid, E., Walster, E. & Bohrnstedt, G. (1973). The body image report. *Psychology Today*, 7, 119–131.

Berscheid, E., Walster, E. & Walster, G. W. (1971). Physical attractiveness and dating choice: A test on the matching hypothesis. *Journal of Experimental Social Psychology*, 7, 173–189.

Betz, N. & Fitzgerald, L. (Eds.). (1987). *The Career Psychology of Women*. Orlando: Academic Press.

Blau, P. M. (1964). *Exchange and Power in Social Life*. New York: John Wiley and Sons.

Blee, K. & Tickamyer, A. (1987). Black-white differences in mother-to-daughter transmission of sex-role attitudes. *The Sociological Quarterly*, 28, 204–222.

Bond, J. R. & Vinacke, W. E. (1961). Coalitions in mixed-sex triads. *Sociometry*, 24, 61–75.

Bowen, G. (1989). Marital sex role incongruence and marital adjustment. *Journal of Family Issues*, 10, 409–415.

Bowen, G. & Orthner, D. (1983). Sex-role congruency and marital quality. *Journal of Marriage and the Family*, 45, 223–230.

Brandwein, R. A., Brown, C. A. & Fox, E. M. (1974). Women and children last: The social situation of divorced mothers and their families. *Journal of Marriage and the Family*, 36, 498–514.

Brehm, M. & Black, W. (1968). Self image and attitudes towards drugs. *Journal of Personality*, 36, 299–314.

Brown, P. & Manela, R. (1978). Changing family roles: Women and divorce. *Journal of Divorce*, 1, 315–328.

Brubaker, T. H. (1990). Families in later life: A burgeoning research area. *Journal of Marriage and the Family*, 52, 959–981.

Brubaker, T. H. (1985). Responsibility for household tasks: A look at golden anniversary couples aged 75 years and older. In W. A. Peterson and J. Quadagno (Eds.), *Social Bonds in Later Life*. Beverly Hills: Sage.

Brubaker, T. H. & Hennon, C. B. (1982). Responsibility for household tasks: Comparing dual-earner and dual-retired marriages. In M. Szinovacz (Ed.), *Women's Retirement*. Beverly Hills: Sage.

Buehler, C., Hogan, M., Robinson, B. & Levy, R. (1985/86). The parental divorce transition: Divorce-related stressors and well-being. *Journal of Divorce*, 9, 61–81.

Burke, R. J. & Weir, T. (1976). Relationship of wives' employment status to husband, wife and pair satisfaction and performance. *Journal of Marriage and the Family*, 38, 279–287.

Burke, R. J., Weir, T. & DuWors, R. (1980). Work demands on administrators and spouse well-being. *Human Relations*, 33, 253–278.

Callan, Victor J. (1987). The personal and marital adjustment of mothers and of voluntarily and involuntarily childless wives. *Journal of Marriage and the Family*, 49, 847–856.

Campbell, A., Converse, P. & Rodgers, W. (1976). *The Quality of American Life*. New York: Russell Sage.

Campbell, M., Steffen, J. J. & Langmeyer, D. (1981). Psychological androgyny and social competence. *Psychological Reports*, 48, 611–614.

Cate, R. M., Lloyd, S. A., Henton, J. M. & Larson, J. H. (1982). Fairness and reward level as predictors of relationship satisfaction. *Social Psychology Quarterly*, 45, 177–81.

Cavior, N. & Boblett, P. J. (1972). Physical attractiveness of dating versus married couples. *Proceedings of the 80th Annual Convention of the American Psychological Association*, 7, 175–176.

Chafetz, J. (1978). *Masculine Feminine or Human?* Itasca, Ill.: Peacock.

Chambers, V. J., Christiansen, J. R. & Kunz, P. R. (1983). Physiognomic homogamy: A test of physical similarity as a factor in the mate selection process. *Social Biology*, 30, 151–157.

Clark, M. & Anderson, B. (1967). *Culture and Aging: An Anthropological Study of Older Americans*. Springfield, Ill.: Charles C. Thomas.

Clark, M. S. & Mills, J. (1979). Interpersonal attraction in exchange and communal relationships. *Journal of Personality and Social Psychology*, 37, 12–24.

Cohen, P., Johnson, J., Lewis, S. & Brook, J. (1990). Single parenthood and employment: Double jeopardy? In J. Eckenrode and S. Gore (Eds.), *Stress Between Work and Family*. New York: Plenum.

Condie, S. (1989). Older married couples. In S. Bahr and E. Peterson (Eds.), *Aging and the Family*. Lexington, Mass.: Lexington Books.

Cook, E. P. (1985). *Psychological Androgyny*. New York: Pergamon Press.

Cooley, C. H. (1902). *Human Nature and the Social Order*. New York: Scribners.

Cooper, K. & Gutmann, D. (1987). Gender identity and ego mastery style in middle-aged, pre- and post-empty nest women. *The Gerontologist*, 27, 347–352.

Crawford, M. P. (1971). Retirement and disengagement. *Human Relations*, 24, 255–278.

Crohan, S. E. & Veroff, J. (1989). Dimensions of marital well-being among white and black newlyweds. *Journal of Marriage and the Family*, 51, 373–383.

Crosby, F. (1982). *Relative Deprivation and Working Women*. New York: Oxford University Press.

Cross, B., Herrmann, R. O. & Warland, R. H. (1975). Effects of family life cycle stage on concerns about food selection. *Journal of the American Dietetic Association*, 67, 131–134.

Crouter, A. C., Perry-Jenkins, M., Huston, T. & McHale, S. (1987). Processes underlying father involvement in dual-earner and single-earner families. *Developmental Psychology*, 23, 431–440.

Cunningham, J. & Antill, J. (1984). Changes in masculinity and femininity across the family life cycle: A reexamination. *Developmental Psychology*, 20, 1135–1141.

Curtis, R. F. (1986). Household and family theory on inequity. *American Sociological Review*, 51, 168–183.

Dambrot, F., Papp, M. & Whitmore, C. (1984). The sex-role attitudes of three generations of women. *Personality and Social Psychology Bulletin*, 10, 469–473.

Davidson, B. (1984). A test of equity theory for marital adjustment. *Social Psychology Quarterly*, 47, 36–42.

Davis, M. S. (1973). *Intimate Relations*. New York: The Free Press.

Derogatis, S. R., Lipman, R. S., Covi, L. & Rickles, K. (1971). Neurotic symptom dimensions. *Archives of General Psychiatry*, 24, 454–464.

Dobson, C. (1983). Sex-role and marital-role expectations. In T. Brubaker (Ed.), *Family Relationships in Later Life*. Beverly Hills: Sage.

Dorfman, L. & Heckert, D. (1988). Egalitarianism in retired rural couples: Household tasks, decision making, and leisure activities. *Family Relations*, 37, 73–78.

Dorris, H. L. & Regaux, B. P. (1974). Perception of marital roles in decision processes. *Journal of Consumer Research*, 1, 51–62.

Downey, A. (1984). The relationship of sex-role orientation to self-perceived health status in middle-aged males. *Sex Roles*, 11, 211–225.

Duncan, B. & Duncan, O. D. (1978). *Sex Typing and Social Roles: A Research Report*. New York: Academic Press.

Emnons, C. A., Biernat, M., Tiedje, L. B., Lang, E. L. & Wortman, C. B. (1990). Stress, support and coping among women professionals with preschool children. In J. Eckenrode and S. Gore (Eds.), *Stress Between Work and Family*. New York: Plenum.

Erdwins, C., Small, A. & Gross, R. (1980). The relationship of self role to self concept. *Journal of Clinical Psychology*, 36, 111–115.

Erdwins, C., Tyer, Z. & Mellinger, J. (1983). A comparison of sex role and related personality traits in young, middle-aged, and older women. *International Journal of Aging and Human Development*, 17, 141–151.

Etaugh, C. & Malstrom, J. (1981). The effect of marital status on person perception. *Journal of Marriage and the Family*, 43, 801–805.

Farkas, G. (1976). Education, wage rates, and division of labor between husbands and wives. *Journal of Marriage and the Family*, 3, 473–484.

Felmlee, D., Sprecher, S. & Bassin, E. (1990). The dissolution of intimate relationships: A hazard model. *Social Psychology Quarterly*, 53, 13–30.

Ferree, M. M. (1988). Negotiating household roles and responsibilities: Resistance, conflict, and change. Paper presented at the annual meeting of the National Council on Family Relations, Philadelphia.

Fieldhouse, P. (1986). *Food and Nutrition: Custom and Culture*. London: Croom Helm.

Fogarty, M., Rapoport, R. & Rapoport, R. (1971). *Sex, Career, and Family*. London: Allen and Unwin.

Fox, K. & Nickols, S. Y. (1983). The time crunch: Wife's employment and family work. *Journal of Family Issues*, 4, 61–82.

Frank, S. J., Towell, P. A. & Huyck, M. (1985). The effects of sex-role traits on three aspects of psychological well-being in a sample of middle-aged women. *Sex Roles*, 12, 1073–1087.

Friedman, H. S. (1976). Effects of self-esteem and expected duration of interaction on liking for a highly rewarding partner. *Journal of Personality and Social Psychology*, 33, 686–690.

Fry, C. (1983). Temporal and status dimensions of life cycles. *International Journal of Aging and Human Development*, 17, 281–300.

Gerber, G. (1987). Sex stereotypes among American college students: Implications for marital happiness, social desirability, and marital power. *Genetic, Social, and General Psychology Monographs*, 113, 4, 413–431.

Gongla, P. & Thompson, E. (1987). Single-parent families. In M. Sussman and S. Steinmetz (Eds.), *Handbook of Marriage and the Family*. New York: Plenum.

Gove, W. & Zeiss, C. (1987). Multiple roles and happiness. In F. Crosby (Ed.), *Spouse, Parent, Worker*. New Haven: Yale University Press.

Griffith, R. W. & Kunz, P. R. (1973). Physiognomic homogamy. *Social Biology*, 20, 448–453.

Gutmann, D. L. (1980). Psychoanalysis and aging: A developmental view. In S. I. Greenspan and G. H. Pollack (Eds.) *The Cause of life: Psychoanalytic Contributions toward Understanding Personality Development*. Vol. III. Washington, D. C.: National Institute of Mental Health.

Gutmann, D. L. (1975). Parenthood: A key to the comparative study of the life cycle. In N. Datan and L. Ginsberg (Eds.), *Life-Span Developmental Psychology*. New York: Academic Press.

Hardesty, C. & Bokemeier, J. (1989). Finding time and making do: Distribution of household labor in nonmetropolitan marriages. *Journal of Marriage and the Family*, 51, 253–267.

Hartmann, H. (1981). The family as the locus of gender, class and political struggle: The example of housework. *Signs*, 6, 366–394.

Hatfield, E. (1978). Global Measure. Reported in E. Hatfield, M.K. Utne, and J. Traupman, Equity Theory and Intimate Relationships. In R. L. Burgess and T. L. Huston (eds.). *Social Exchange in Developing Relationships*. New York: Academic Press.

Hatfield, E. & Sprecher, S. (1986). *Mirror Mirror*. Albany: State University of New York Press.

Hatfield, E. & Traupmann, J. (1981). Intimate relationships: A perspective from equity theory. In S. Duck and R. Gilmour (Eds.), *Personal Relationships*. 1: *Studying Personal Relationships*. New York: Academic Press.

Helmick, S. A. (1978). Family living patterns: Projection for the future. *Journal of Nutritional Education*, 10, 4.

Hertzler, A. A. & Schulman, R. S. (1983). Employed women, dieting, and support groups. *Journal of American Dietetic Association*, 82, 153–158.

Hertzler, A. A. & Vaughan, C. E. (1979). The relationship of family structure and interaction to nutrition. *Journal of American Dietetic Association*, 73, 23–27.

Herzog, R. A. & Bachman, J. G. (1986). Sex role attitudes among high school seniors: Views about work and family roles. *ISR Newsletter*, 10, 1–2. Ann Arbor: University of Michigan Institute for Social Research.

Hill, C. T., Rubin, Z. & Peplau, L. A. (1976). Breakups before marriage: The end of 103 affairs. *Journal of Social Issues*, 32, 147–168.

Hiller, D. V. & Philliber, W. W. (1986). The division of labor in contemporary marriage: Expectations, perceptions, and performance. *Social Problems*, 33, 191–201.

Hinchcliffe, M. K., Hooper, D. & Roberts, F. J. (1978). *The Melancholy Marriage*. Chichester, England: John Wiley and Sons.

Hoffman, L. & Nye, I. (Eds.), (1975). *Working Mothers*. San Francisco: Jossey-Bass.

Homans, G. C. (1974). *Social Behavior: Its Elementary Forms*. Revised Edition. New York: Harcourt, Brace & World.

Huber, J. & Spitze, G. (1983). *Sex Stratification: Children, Housework and Jobs*. New York: Academic Press.

Huber, J. & Spitze, G. (1981). Wives' employment, household behaviors and sex-role attitudes. *Social Forces*, 60, 150–169.

Hyde, J. S. & Phillis, D. E. (1979). Androgyny across the life-span. *Developmental Psychology*, 15, 334–336.

Ingham, J. G., Kreitman, N. B., Miller, P. M., Sashidharan, S. P. & Surtees, P. G. (1986). Self-esteem, vulnerability and psychiatric disorder in the community. *British Journal of Psychiatry*, 148, 375–385.

Johnson, P. J. (1986). Divorced mothers: Sources of support for conflicts in responsibilities: *Journal of Divorce*, 9, 89–105.

Jones, S. C., Knurek, D. A. & Regan, D. T. (1973). Variables affecting reactions to social acceptance and rejection. *Journal of Social Psychology*, 90, 269–284.

Jones, W. H., Chernovetz, M. E. & Hansson, R. O. (1978). The enigma of androgyny: Differential implications for males and females? *Journal of Consulting and Clinical Psychology*, 46, 298–313.

Kalick, S. M. & Hamilton, T. E. (1986). The matching hypothesis reexamined. *Journal of Personality and Social Psychology*, 4, 673–682.

Kamo, Y. (1988). Determinants of the household division of labor: Resources, power, and ideology. *Journal of Family Issues*, 9, 177–200.

Keating, N. & Cole, P. (1980). What do I do with him 24 hours a day? Changes in the housewife role after retirement. *The Gerontologist*, 20, 84–89.

Keith, P. (1989). *The Unmarried in Later Life*. New York: Praeger.

Keith, P. (1985a). Changing patterns and life satisfaction. In E. Powers, W. Goudy, and P. Keith (Eds.), *Later Life Transitions*. Boston: Kluwer-Nijhoff.

Keith, P. (1985b). Importance of life areas. In E. Powers, W. Goudy, and P. Keith (Eds.), *Later Life Transitions*. Boston: Kluwer-Nijhoff.

Keith, P. (1980). Sex differences in household involvement of the unmarried. *Journal of Gerontological Social Work*, 2, 331–343.

Keith, P., Dobson, C., Goudy, W. & Powers, E. (1981). Older men. *Journal of Family Issues*, 2, 336–349.

Keith, P. & Lorenz, F. (1989). Financial strain and health of unmarried older people. *The Gerontologist*, 29, 684–691.

Keith, P., Powers, E. & Goudy, W. (1981). Older men in employed and retired families. *Alternative Lifestyles*, 4, 228–241.

Keith, P. & Schafer, R. (1986). Housework, disagreement, and depression among younger and older couples. *American Behavioral Scientist*, 29, 405–422.

Keith, P. & Schafer, R. (1983). Employment characteristics of both spouses and depression in one and two-job families. *Journal of Marriage and the Family*, 45, 877–884.

Keith, P. & Schafer, R. (1980). Role strain and depression in two-job families. *Family Relations*, 29, 483–488.

Kerckhoff, A. (1966). Husband-wife expectations and reactions to retirement. In I. H. Simpson and J. McKinney (Eds.), *Social Aspects of Aging*. Durham, N.C.: Duke University Press.

Kessler, R. & McRae, J. (1982). The effect of wives' employment on the mental health of married men and women. *American Sociological Review*, 47, 216–227.

Kinch, J. W. (1963). A formalized theory of the self-concept. *American Journal of Sociology*, 90, 269–284.

Kline, R. L. & Terry, R. D. (1986). Differences in beliefs about heart disease risk factors between men and women. *Journal of American Dietetic Association*, 86, 786–788.

Kramer, L. (1991). *The Sociology of Gender*. New York: St. Martin's Press.

Kreckel, M. (1982). Communicative acts and shared knowledge: A conceptual framework and its empirical application. *Semiotica*, 40, 45–88.

Kremer, Y. (1985). Parenthood and marital role performance among retired workers: Comparison between pre- and post-retirement period. *Ageing and Society*, 5, 449–460.

Lane, I. M. & Messe, L. A. (1971). Equity and the distribution of rewards. *Journal of Personality and Social Psychology*, 20 (October), 1–17.

Levinger, G. (1983). Development and change. In H.H. Kelley, E. Berscheid, A.

Christensen, J. H. Harvey, T.H. Huston, G. Levinger, E. McClintock, L. Peplau, and D. Peterson (Eds.), *Close Relationships*. New York: W.H. Freeman.

Lewin, K. (1943). Forces behind food habits and methods of change. In *The Problem of Changing Food Habits*. Washington, D.C.: National Academy of Sciences Bulletin 198.

Lewis, S. & Cooper, C. (1987). Stress in dual-earner families. *Women and Work*, 3, 139–168.

Li, J. & Caldwell, R. (1987). Magnitude and directional effects of marital sex-role incongruence on marital adjustment. *Journal of Family Issues*, 8, 97–110.

Libby, W. L. & Yaklevich, D. (1973). Personality determinants of eye contact and gaze aversion. *Journal of Personality and Social Psychology*, 27, 197–206.

Lipman, A. (1961). Role conceptions and morale of couples in retirement. *Journal of Gerontology*, 16, 267–271.

Lipman, A. (1960). Marital roles of the retired aged. *Merrill-Palmer Quarterly of Behavior and Development*, 6, 192–195.

Livson, F. B. (1983). Changing sex roles in the social environment of later life. In G. D. Rowles and R. J. Ohta (Eds.), *Aging and Milieu: Environmental Perspectives in Growing Old*. New York: Academic Press.

Lopata, H. Z., Barnewalt, D. & Norr, K. (1980). *Dual-Career Couples*. Beverly Hills, Calif.: Sage Publications.

Losh-Hesselbart, S. (1987). Development of gender roles. In M. Sussman and S. Steinmetz (Eds.), *Handbook of Marriage and the Family*. New York: Plenum.

Luck, P. W. & Heiss, J. (1972). Social determinants of self esteem in adult males. *Sociology and Social Research*, 57, 69–84.

Mangus, S. R. (1957). Role theory and marriage counseling. *Social Forces*, 35 (March), 200–209.

Mattessich, P. & Hill, R. (1987). Life Cycle and Family Development. In M. Sussman and S. Steinmetz (Eds.), *Handbook of Marriage and the Family*. New York: Plenum.

Maxine, B. Z. & Eitzen, D. S. (1987). *Diversity in American Families*. New York: Harper & Row Publishers.

McBroom, W. H. (1986). Changes in role orientations of women: A study of sex role traditionalism over a five-year period. *Journal of Family Issues*, 7, 149–159.

McGee, J. & Wells, K. (1982). Gender typing and androgyny in later life. *Human Development*, 25, 116–139.

McKillip, J. & Riedle, S. S. (1983). External validity of matching on physical attractiveness for same and opposite sex couples. *Journal of Applied Social Psychology*, 13, 328–337.

Mead, G. H. (1934). *Mind, Self and Society*. Chicago: University of Chicago Press.

Menaghan, E. (1985). Depressive affect and subsequent divorce. *Journal of Family Issues*, 6, 295–306.

Menaghan, E. (1983). Marital stress and family transitions: A panel analysis. *Journal of Marriage and the Family*, 45, 371–386.

Metropolitan Life Insurance Company. (1983). *1983 Metropolitan Height and Weight Tables*. New York: Metropolitan Life Insurance Co.

Michaels, J. W., Acock, A. C. & Edwards, J. N. (1986). Social exchange and equity determinants of relationship commitment. *Journal of Social and Personal Relationships*, 31, 61–75.

Michaels, J. W., Edwards, J. N. & Acock, A. C. (1984). Satisfaction in intimate relationships as a function of inequality, inequity and outcomes. *Social Psychology Quarterly*, 47, 347–57.

Mirowsky, J. (1985). Depression and marital power: An equity model. *American Journal of Sociology*, 91, 557–592.

Model, S. (1981). Housework by husbands: Determinants and implications. *Journal of Family Issues*, 2, 225–237.

Morgan, C. S., Affleck, M. & Riggs, L. R. (1986). Gender, personality traits, and depression. *Social Science Quarterly*, 67, 69–83.

Morgan, W. R. & Sawyer, J. (1967). Bargaining, expectations and the preference for equality over equity. *Journal of Personality and Social Psychology*, 6 (June), 139–149.

Mortimer, J. (1980). Occupation-family linkages as perceived by men in the early stages of professional and managerial careers. In H. Lopata (Ed.), *Research in the Interweave of Social Roles: Women and Men*. Vol. 1. Greenwich, Conn.: JAI Press.

Mortimer, J., Lorence, J. & Kumka, D. (1986). *Work, Family and Personality: Transition to Adulthood*. Norwood, N.J.: Ablex.

Murstein, B. I. (1976). *Who will marry whom? Theories and research in marital choice*. New York: Springer.

Murstein, B. I. (1972). Physical attractiveness and marital choice. *Journal of Personality and Social Psychology*, 22 (April), 8–12.

Murstein, B. I. & Christy, P. (1976). Physical attractiveness and marriage adjustment in middle age couples. *Journal of Personality and Social Psychology*, 34, 537–542.

Murstein, B. I., Cerreto, M. & MacDonald, M. G. (1977). A theory and investigation of the effect of exchange orientation on marriage and friendship. *Journal of Marriage and the Family*, 39 (August), 543–548.

Nash, S. C. & Feldman, S. S. (1981). Sex role and sex related attributions: Constancy and change across the family life cycle. In M. E. Lamb and A. L. Brown (Eds.), *Advances in Developmental Psychology*, 2. New Jersey: Lea.

National Cancer Institute. Committee on Diet, Nutrition and Cancer. (1982). *Diet, Nutrition and Cancer*. Washington, D.C.: National Academy Press, 1–14.

National Institutes of Health. (1985). Lowering blood cholesterol to prevent heart disease: Consensus conference. *Journal of the American Medical Association*, 253, 2080–2086.

Nickols, S. Y. & Metzer, E. J. (1982). Impact of wife's employment upon husband's housework. *Journal of Family Issues*, 3, 199–216.

Norton, A. & Glick, P. (1986). One parent families: A social and economic profile. *Family Relations*, 35, 9–17.

Nyquist, L., Slivken, K., Spence, J. T. & Helmreich, R. L. (1985). Household responsibilities in middle-class couples: The contribution of demographic and personality variables. *Sex Roles*, 12, 15–34.

O'Kelly, C. G. & Carney, L. S. (1986). *Women and Men in Society*, 2d ed. Belmont, Calif.: Wadsworth Publishing Co.

Orlofsky, J., Cohen, R. & Ramsden, M. (1985). Relationship between sex-role attitudes and personality traits and the revised sex-role behavior scale. *Sex Roles*, 12, 277–391.

Orlofsky, J. & Windle, M. (1978). Sex role orientation, behavioral adaptability and personal adjustment. *Sex Roles*, 4, 801–811.

O'Toole, J. (Ed.). (1975). *Work in America*. Cambridge: MIT Press.

Pearce, W. & Cronen, V. (1980). *Communication Action and Meaning*. New York: Praeger.

Pearlin, L. I. (1975). Sex roles and depression. In N. Datan and L. Ginsberg (Eds.), *Proceedings of Fourth Life Span Developmental Psychology Conference: Normative Life Crises*. New York: Academic Press.

Pearlin, L. I. & Johnson, J. S. (1977). Marital status, life strains and depression. *American Sociological Review*, 42, 704–715.

Pederson, D. M. & Breglio, V. J. (1968). Personality correlates of actual self-disclosure. *Psychological Reports*, 22, 495–501.

Peterson, R. (1989). *Women, Work, and Divorce*. Albany: State University of New York.

Piotrkowski, C., Rapoport, R. & Rapoport, R. (1987). Families and work. In M. Sussman and S. Steinmetz (Eds.), *Handbook of Marriage and the Family*. New York: Plenum.

Pleck, J. H. (1985). *Working Wives/Working Husbands*. Beverly Hills: Sage.

Pleck, J. H. (1983). Husbands' paid work and family roles: Current research issues. In H. Lopata and J. Pleck (Eds.), *Research in the Interweave of Social Roles: Families and Jobs*, 3, 251–333. Greenwich, Conn.: JAI Press.

Pleck, J. H., Stains, G. & Long, L. (1980). Conflicts between work and family life. *Monthly Labor Review*, 168, 29–31.

Price, R. & Vandenberg, S. (1980). Spouse similarity in American and Swedish couples. *Behavior Genetics*, 10, 59–71.

Prithard, R. D., Dunnette, M. D. & Jorgenson, D. O. (1972). Effects of perceptions of equity and inequity on worker performance and satisfaction. *Journal of Applied Psychology Monograph*, 56, 75–94.

Puglisi, J. (1983). Self-perceived age changes in sex role self concept. *International Journal of Aging and Human Development*, 16, 183–191.

Quinn, R. P. (1978). Physical deviance and occupational mistreatment: The short, the fat and the ugly. Master's Thesis, University of Michigan Survey Research Center, University of Michigan, Ann Arbor.

Quinn, W. & Davidson, B. (1986). Marital type and the marriage relationship. *Marriage and Family Review*, 10, 117–131.

Rapoport, R. (1964). Transition from engagement to marriage. *Acta Sociologica*, 17, 35–56.

Rapoport, R. & Rapoport, R. N. (1965). Work and family in contemporary society. *American Sociological Review*, 30 (June), 381–394.

Rapoport, R. & Rapoport, R. N. (1975). *Leisure and the Family Life Cycle*. London: Routledge and Kegan Paul.

Rexroat, C. & Shehan, C. (1987). The family life cycle and spouses' time in housework. *Journal of Marriage and the Family*, 49, 737–750.

Rosenberg, M. (1981). The self-concept: Social product and social force. In M. Rosenberg and R.H. Turner (Eds.), *Social Psychology: Sociological Perspectives*. New York: Basic Books.

Rosenberg, M. (1979). *Conceiving the Self*. New York: Basic Books.

Rosenfield, S. (1980). Sex differences in depression: Do women always have higher rates? *Journal of Health and Social Behavior*, 21, 33–42.

Ross, C. (1987). The division of labor at home. *Social Forces*, 65, 816–833.

Ross, C., Mirowsky, J. & Huber, J. (1983). Dividing work, sharing work, and in-between: Marriage patterns and depression. *American Sociological Review*, 48, 809–823.

Rubin, Z. (1973). *Liking and Loving: An Invitation to Social Psychology*. New York: Holt.

Rusbult, C. E., Morrow, G. D. & Johnson, D. J. (1987). Self-esteem and problem-solving behavior in close relationships. *British Journal of Social Psychology*, 26, 293–303.

Sabatelli, R. M. & Cecil-Pigo, E. F. (1985). Relational interdependence and commitment in marriage. *Journal of Marriage and the Family*, 47, 931–37.

Sanjur, D. (1982). *Social and Cultural Perspectives in Nutrition*. Englewood Cliffs, N.J.: Prentice-Hall.

Sawyer, J. (1966). The Altruism Scale: A measure of cooperative, individualistic and competitive interpersonal orientation. *American Journal of Sociology*, 71, 409–430.

Scanzoni, J. (1980). Contemporary marriage types. *Journal of Family Issues*, 1, 125–140.

Scanzoni, J. & Arnett, C. (1987). Policy implications derived from a study of rural and urban marriages. *Family Relations*, 36, 430–436.

Schafer, E. (1985). Cardiovascular disease risk factors in an Iowa population. Diet Therapy U.S.A. Conference, Iowa City, Iowa.

Schafer, R. B. (1978). Factors affecting food behavior and the quality of husbands' and wives' diets. *Journal of American Dietetic Association*, 72, 138–143.

Schafer, R. B. & Braito, R. (1979). Self-concept and role performance evaluation among marriage partners. *Journal of Marriage and the Family*, 4, 801–810.

Schafer, R. B. & Schafer, E. A. (1989). Relationship Between Gender and Food Roles in the Family. *Journal of Nutrition Education*, 21, 119–126.

Seidenberg, R. (1973). *Corporate Wives—Corporate Casualties?* New York: Doubleday.

Sharpley, C. F. & Kahn, J. A. (1980). Self-concept, value systems and marital adjustment: Some implications for marriage counselors. *International Journal for the Advancement of Counseling*, 3, 137–145.

Sherwood, J. J. (1962). Self identity and self actualization: A theory and research. Ph.D. dissertation, University of Michigan, Ann Arbor.

Shichman, S. & Cooper, E. (1984). Life satisfaction and sex-role concept. *Sex Roles*, 11, 227–240.

Shorkey, C. T. (1980). Sense of personal worth, self esteem and anomia of child abusing mothers and controls. *Journal of Clinical Psychology*, 36, 817–820.

Sieber, S. (1974). Toward a theory of role accumulation. *American Sociological Review*, 39, 567–578.

Sinnott, J. D. (1986). *Sex Roles and Aging: Theory and Research from a Systems Perspective*. Basel and New York: Karger.

Sinnott, J. D. (1984). Older men, older women: Are their perceived sex roles similar? *Sex Roles*, 10, 847–856.

Sinnott, J. D. (1982). Correlates of sex roles of older adults. *Journal of Gerontology*, 37, 587–594.

Spanier, G. B. & Hanson, S. (1981). The role of extended kin in the adjustment to marital separation. *Journal of Divorce*, 5, 33–48.

Spence, J. T., Helmreich, R. & Stapp, J. (1975). Ratings of self and peers on sex role attributes and their relation to self-esteem and conceptions of masculinity and femininity. *Journal of Personality and Social Psychology*, 32, 29–39.

Spitze, G. (1988). Women's employment and family relations: A review. *Journal of Marriage and the Family*, 50, 595–618.

Sprecher, S. (1986). The relation between inequity and emotions in close relationships. *Social Psychology Quarterly*, 49, 309–21.

Statistical Abstract of the United States. (1990). Washington, D.C.: Government Printing Office.

Stephen, T. D. (1985). Fixed-sequences and circular-causal models of relationship development: Divergent views of the role of communication in intimacy. *Journal of Marriage and the Family*, 47, 955–963.

Storr, A. (1979). *The Art of Psychotherapy*. London: Şecker & Warburg.

Swanson-Rudd, J., Fox, H., Crumley, W., Doyle, M., Johnson, N. & Nerull, K. (1983). Nutrition orientations of working mothers in the North Central Region. *Journal of Nutrition Education*, 14, 132–133.

Szinovacz, M. (1989). Retirement, couples, and household work. In S. Bahr and E. Peterson (Eds.), *Aging and the Family*. Lexington, Mass.: Lexington Books.

Szinovacz, M. (1984). Changing family roles and interactions. *Marriage and Family Review*, 7, 163–201.

Szinovacz, M. (1983). Beyond the hearth: Older women and retirement. In E. Markson (Ed.), *Older Women*. Lexington, Mass.: Lexington Books.

Szinovacz, M. (1980). Female retirement: Effects on spousal roles and marital adjustment. *Journal of Family Issues*, 1, 423–440.

Thibaut, J. & Kelley, H. (1959). *The Social Psychology of Groups*. New York: John Wiley.

Thoits, P. (1987). Negotiating roles. In F. Crosby (Ed.), *Spouse, Parent, Worker*. New Haven: Yale University Press.

Thomas, D. A. & Reznikoff, M. (1984). Sex role orientation, personality structure, and adjustment in women. *Journal of Personality Assessment*, 48, 28–36.

Thompson, L. & Walker, A. (1989). Gender in families: Women and men in marriage, work and parenthood. *Journal of Marriage and the Family*, 51, 845–871.

Treas, J. & Bengtson, V. (1987). The family in later years. In M. Sussman and S. Steinmetz (Eds.), *Handbook of Marriage and the Family*. New York: Plenum.

Utne, M. K., Hatfield, E., Traupmann, J. & Greenberger, D. (1984). Equity, marital satisfaction, and stability. *Journal of Social and Personal Relationships*, 1, 323–32.

Verbrugge, L. (1987). Role responsibilities, role burdens, and physical health. In F. Crosby (Ed.), *Spouse, Parent, Worker*. New Haven, Conn.: Yale University Press.

Veroff, J., Douvan, E. & Kulka, R. (1981). *The Inner American*. New York: Basic Books.

Vinacke, W. E. & Gullickson, G. R. (1964). Age and sex differences in the formation of coalitions. *Child Development*, 35, 1217–1231.

Voydanoff, P. (1988). Work role characteristics, family structure demands, and work/family conflict. *Journal of Marriage and the Family*, 50, 749–761.

Waite, L. J. (1981). *U.S. Women at Work*. Population Bulletin 36(2), 1–43.

Walster, E., Aronson, V., Abrahams, D. & Rottmann, L. (1966). Importance of physical attractiveness in dating behavior. *Journal of Personality and Social Psychology*, 4, 508–516.

Walster, E., Berscheid, E. & Walster, G. W. (1976). New directions in equity research. In Berkowitz and E. Walster (Eds.), *Advances in Experimental Social Psychology*, 9. New York: Academic Press.

Walster, E., Walster, G. W. & Berscheid, E. (1978). *Equity: Theory and Research*. Boston: Allyn and Bacon.

Walster, E., Walster, G. W. & Traupmann, S. (1978). Equity and premarital sex. *Journal of Personality and Social Psychology*, 36, 82–92.

Whicker, M. & Kronenfeld, J. (1986). *Sex Role Changes*. New York: Praeger.

Whisman, M. & Jacobson, N. (1989). Depression and marital satisfaction and marital and personality measures of sex-roles. *Journal of Marital and Family Therapy*, 15, 177–186.

White, G. S. (1981). Some correlates of romantic jealousy. *Journal of Personality*, 49, 129–147.

White, G. S. (1980). Physical attractiveness and courtship progress. *Journal of Personality and Social Psychology*, 39, 82–92.

Whitley, B. E., Jr. (1984). Sex-role orientation and psychological well-being: Two meta-analyses. *Sex Roles*, 12, 207–225.

Windle, M. (1986). Sex role orientation, cognitive flexibility, and life satisfaction among older adults. *Psychology of Women Quarterly*, 10, 263–273.

Windle, M. & Sinnott, J. D. (1985). A psychometric study of the Bem Sex Role Inventory with an older adult sample. *Journal of Gerontology*, 40, 336–343.

Zammichieli, M., Gilroy, F. & Sherman, M. (1988). Relation between sex-role orientation and marital satisfaction. *Personality and Social Psychology Bulletin*, 14, 747–754.

Index

ABOUT THE AUTHORS

PAT M. KEITH is Professor of Sociology and Assistant Dean in the Graduate College at Iowa State University, Ames, Iowa. She has published numerous articles, coedited *Later Life Transitions*, and recently authored *The Unmarried in Later Life*. Current research includes a study of guardianship of older persons supported by the AARP Andrus Foundation.

ROBERT B. SCHAFER is a Professor in the Department of Sociology and Anthropology at Iowa State University, Ames, Iowa. He received his Ph.D. from the Pennsylvania State University. He has conducted research and published in the areas of family and social psychology. He has received the J. H. Ellis award for excellence in teaching.